THE NEW MERMAIDS

'Tis Pity She's a Whore

THE NEW MERMAIDS

General Editor
BRIAN GIBBONS
Professor of English Literature, University of Zürich

Previous General Editors
PHILIP BROCKBANK
BRIAN MORRIS
ROMA GILL

'Tis Pity She's a Whore

JOHN FORD

Edited by
BRIAN MORRIS
Principal, St. David's University College
Lampeter

LONDON/A. & C. BLACK

NEW YORK/W. W. NORTON

Reprinted 1986
by A. & C. Black (Publishers) Limited
35 Bedford Row, London WC1 4JH

First published in this form 1968
by Ernest Benn Limited

Fourth impression 1986

© *Ernest Benn Limited 1968*

Published in the United States of America by
W. W. Norton and Company, Inc.
500 Fifth Avenue, New York, N.Y. 10110

Printed in Great Britain

British Library Cataloguing in Publication Data

Ford, John, b. ca 1586
  'Tis pity she's a whore.—(The new mermaids).
  I. Title II. Morris, Brian III. Series
  822'.3   PR2524.T5

ISBN 0-7136-2833-2
ISBN 0-393-90011 8 (U.S.A.)

CONTENTS

v

ACKNOWLEDGEMENTS

THE STANDARD edition of Ford is still *The Works of John Ford*, edited by Gifford and revised by Dyce (1869), and all Ford's editors are in its debt. I have also made use of Havelock Ellis's original *Mermaid* edition (1888), Sherman's edition of *'Tis Pity She's a Whore* and *The Broken Heart*, Boston and London, 1915, de Vocht's reprint, Louvain, 1927, McIlwraith's edition in *Five Stuart Tragedies*, The World's Classics, Oxford, 1953, and N. W. Bawcutt's edition in the Regents Renaissance Drama Series, 1966, which is by far the most scholarly and intelligent edition. For considerable enlightenment on the theme of the play I am indebted to some striking discussions with my colleagues Mrs Elizabeth Irvine, Mr Norman Rea, and Mr Bernard Harris. Professor Philip Brockbank has watched benignly over all.

INTRODUCTION

THE AUTHOR

Deep In a dumpe Iacke forde alone was gott
Wth folded Armes and Melancholye hatt,
(William Hemminge, *Elegy on Randolph's Finger*)

JOHN FORD was baptized at Ilsington, Devonshire, on 17 April 1586. Nothing is known of his early years, or his education, but he was admitted to the Middle Temple on 16 November 1602. Several of his relations were already members, and others followed him there. In the Hilary Term of 1605–6 he was expelled for failing to pay his buttery bill (a common offence) and was not re-admitted until 10 June 1608. He was certainly resident thereafter until 1617, and probably practised law in some capacity, though the records show that he was never called to the bar. From 1606 on he published several small works in prose and verse, but there is no certain evidence that he wrote anything for the stage before 1621. Between 1621 and 1625 he collaborated with Thomas Dekker and others in at least five plays, including *The Witch of Edmonton* and the masque, *The Sun's Darling*. After 1625 Ford probably worked alone. He contributed commendatory verses to plays by Webster, Shirley, Massinger, Brome and others, and a poem to the memorial volume for Ben Jonson, *Jonsonus Virbius*. His three greatest plays, *'Tis Pity She's a Whore*, *The Broken Heart*, and *Perkin Warbeck*, belong to the period 1625–34, when Ford was writing first for the King's Company and then for Christopher Beeston's companies at the Phoenix. The last of his plays known to have been produced in his lifetime is *The Lady's Trial* (early summer 1638) and nothing is known of Ford's life after that date. It was published early in 1639 with prefatory matter by the dramatist, and it is generally assumed that he died soon after.[1]

DATE AND SOURCES

The play was first published in 1633, and the title-page of this edition declares 'Acted by the Queenes Maiesties Seruants, at the Phoenix in Drury-Lane'. The Queen's Company was formed in

[1] See M. J. Sargeaunt, *John Ford*, Oxford, 1935, 1–31, and G. E. Bentley, *The Jacobean and Caroline Stage*, Oxford, 1941–56, iii, 433 ff.

1626, and Bentley argues that Ford's plays for the Phoenix theatre were probably written after the plays he wrote for the King's men at Blackfriars, which would suggest a date of 1629–33.[2] He points out that some slight support for a performance date shortly before publication is provided by the printer's apology at the end of the Quarto:

> The generall Commendation deserued by the Actors, in their Presentment of this Tragedy, may easily excuse such few faults, as are escaped in the Printing.

In the dedication to the Earl of Peterborough Ford writes 'Your Noble allowance of These *First Fruites* of my leasure in the Action, emboldens my confidence . . .' and this phrase has given rise to a great deal of conjecture. Some have taken it to mean that this is Ford's first independent play. It is impossible to say with any certainty either what the 'first fruites' are, or what period of leisure he might be talking about. The evidence is inconclusive. The only other speculation has been Sherman's suggestion[3] that the theme was suggested to Ford by the trial of Sir Giles Allington, in 1631, for marrying the daughter of his half-sister. But there is nothing in the play itself to suggest that Ford knew the case.

No source for the play has been discovered. A strong case has been put by Sherman for believing that Ford knew Sperone Speroni's play, *Canace e Macareo* (1546), but what struck Sherman was not a similarity of plot, but a similarity between the two writers in their attitude to incest. Several other analogues have been suggested by different scholars: Rosset's *Histoires Tragiques*, No. 5, Thomas Heywood's *Gunaikeion*, and Tirso de Molina's *La Venganza de Tamar*. But it seems perfectly possible that Ford created the whole story himself.

THE PLAY

> and i you dont believe i am serious and he i think you are too serious to give me any cause for alarm you wouldnt have felt driven to the expedient of telling me you have committed incest otherwise and i i wasnt lying i wasnt lying and he you wanted to sublimate a piece of natural human folly into a horror and then exorcize it with truth and i it was to isolate her out of the loud world so that it would have to flee us of necessity and then the sound of it would be as though it had never been
>
> (Faulkner, *The Sound and the Fury*)

[2] G. E. Bentley, *The Jacobean and Caroline Stage*, Oxford, 1941–56, iii, 463.
[3] S. P. Sherman, ed., *'Tis Pity She's a Whore* and *The Broken Heart*, Boston and London, 1915, p. xxxvi.

Georg Lukacs, writing on the ideology of modernism, instances
Faulkner as an extreme example of what he regards as a major
tendency in modernist literature—the 'attenuation of actuality'. This
tendency

> is carried *ad absurdum* where the stream of consciousness is that of
> an abnormal subject or of an idiot — consider the first part of
> Faulkner's *Sound and Fury* or, a still more extreme case, Beckett's
> *Molloy*.[4]

Lukacs argues that, in modernist literature, this attenuation works to
destroy the complex tissue of man's relations with his environment,
furthers the dissolution of personality, and drives him to take refuge
in psychopathology. At the beginning of this century Alfred Kerr
wrote: 'For what is poetic in everyday life? Neurotic aberration,
escape from life's dreary routine. Only in this way can a character be
translated to a rarer clime and yet retain an air of reality.'[5] In such a
climate of opinion it might well be thought that Ford's *'Tis Pity*
must take its place alongside Joyce, Kafka, and Musil as a significant
document in a cultural decadence. It is centrally concerned with
incestuous love, its hero, Giovanni, behaves, by the end of the play,
in a completely psychopathic way, it isolates characters from their
environment, it displays the disintegration of personality. Yet I
believe that *'Tis Pity* is essentially a realist play, concerned to report
objectively upon an egregious aspect of human behaviour, to open
the correct social perspective, to avoid distortion, and to reflect
reality truthfully. My claim for the contemporary importance of the
play rests upon the sensitivity of modern society to questions of the
deepest human relationships, and the sense that love and law are not
always coterminous.

NATURAL HUMAN FOLLY

'Tis Pity may or may not have been an 'occasional' play. S. P.
Sherman suggested in his edition[6] that Ford may have been influenced in his choice of a theme by the case of Sir Giles Allington,
who, in 1631, two years before the publication of *'Tis Pity*, was
heavily fined in the ecclesiastical court 'for intermarrying with
Dorothy Dalton, daughter of Michael Dalton and his wife, which
latter was half-sister to Sir Giles'.[7] Joseph Mead, reporting on the

---

[4] Georg Lukacs, *The Meaning of Contemporary Realism*, trans. J. and N.
Mander, 1963, p. 26.
[5] Quoted by Lukacs, p. 28.
[6] *'Tis Pity She's a Whore* and *The Broken Heart*, ed. S. P. Sherman, Boston
and London, 1915, p. xxxvi.
[7] *Calendar of State Papers, Domestic*, 1631.

trial, wrote: 'It was the solemnest, the gravest and the severest censure that ever, they say, was made in that court.' Whether this influenced Ford or not, plays about incest were by no means uncommon in the period: Tourneur's *Revenger's Tragedy* and *Atheist's Tragedy*, Beaumont and Fletcher's *A King and No King*, Massinger's *The Unnatural Combat*, Middleton's *Women Beware Women*, and Brome's *The Lovesick Court* (1632–40) had all been written since the turn of the century, and all dallied with the forbidden topic to a greater or lesser extent. But *'Tis Pity* is the only play which makes incest its central theme, and explores to the full the nature and consequences of the relationship. The play opens with an abrupt, urgent statement, emphasising the seriousness of the subject and placing it beyond the bounds of rational disputation:

> . . . nice philosophy
> May tolerate unlikely arguments,
> But Heaven admits no jest: wits that presumed
> On wit too much, by striving how to prove
> There was no God, with foolish grounds of art,
> Discovered first the nearest way to hell,
> And filled the world with devilish atheism.   (I, i, 2–8)

The allusion to the intellectual pride which caused the downfall of Dr. Faustus adds a resonance to these otherwise swift, persuasive lines, and sets an immediate cosmic context for the incest question. This opening scene carries complete conviction because the instinctive first reaction, in any age, to the idea of incest seems to have been to condemn it as contrary to the entire order of things. In this scene (if in no other) the Friar is in no doubt about his moral bearings. To all Giovanni's arguments he presents the inflexible reply: 'Have done . . . Repentance . . . blasphemy . . . death waits on thy lust . . . Heaven is just'. The effect is to create a deadlocked opposition between desire and duty, and the responses of the audience are firmly directed into the orthodox moral judgement—what is being suggested is ethically and socially evil and repugnant. Ford does not permit Giovanni convincing arguments with which to assault prejudice; indeed his slightly feverish questions hardly form an argument—to him incest is only a name and a convention, the closer the kin the closer the affection—these attitudes function only to confirm an audience's assumption of what is right and what is wrong in this situation. So powerful is the taboo upon the action in all societies that the person who commits it is felt to be tainted, marked out for some terrible retribution. Weinberg reports a typical reaction from a housewife in present-day America:

The word makes me shudder. I heard of a case that happened but I never saw the people. They both must be insane to do such a thing. Why? It's almost beyond imagination. Only a brute and a fool would think of doing such a thing.[8]

Giovanni, in I, ii, is fully aware of the disruptive force of his incestuous love, and he expresses it in an image which precisely fixes the nature of his torment:

> The love of thee, my sister, and the view
> Of thy immortal beauty hath untuned
> All harmony both of my rest and life.   (I, ii, 212–14)

Annabella's response is in the same grave key, and their sense of the solemnity, the awfulness, of their love is brilliantly captured in the marvellous delicacy of the ritual which follows:

ANNABELLA   On my knees,   *She kneels*
  Brother, even by our mother's dust, I charge you,
  Do not betray me to your mirth or hate,
  Love me, or kill me, brother.
GIOVANNI   On my knees,   *He kneels*
  Sister, even by my mother's dust, I charge you,
  Do not betray me to your mirth or hate,
  Love me, or kill me, sister.   (I, ii, 249–55)

There is a similar scene between Orgilus and Penthea in *The Broken Heart*, II, iii, and it is part of the greatness of Ford's art that the utter simplicity, the 'artlessness' of these self-made rituals, purifies and dedicates whatever passions are involved, as if the participants have become votaries. Yet for all its solemnity the ritual has something in it of a children's game, an invincible innocence out of which Giovanni can ask his sister

> What must we now do?

as if she knew the rules, and he had momentarily forgotten them.

So, by the end of Act I the lovers have established themselves as transgressors, sentient of the nature of their sin and aware of its inevitable outcome. There is no sense of any hysterical defiance of the order of God and man, no search for forbidden experience, no aspiring mind. Giovanni, in particular, has gone through all the formal religious ritual of contrition, fasting, repentance, but it brings him no release. The ineluctable fact remains: two people are deeply in love, but there is a social prohibition which forbids them to marry. They break the taboo.

Giovanni's replacement of religious sanctions with a rather vague idea of fate as controller of his actions ('my fates have doomed my death') lends an almost dreamlike freedom to the conversation

8 S. K. Weinberg, *Incest Behavior*, New York, 1955, p. 29.

between the lovers in II, i. Their love has been consummated, and the
heavens have not fallen. To all outward appearances nothing has
changed:

> I marvel why the chaster of your sex
> Should think this pretty toy called maidenhead
> So strange a loss, when, being lost, 'tis nothing,
> And you are still the same.   (II, i, 9–12)

Again, in a single image, Ford focuses the quality of the moment:

> . . . Thus hung Jove on Leda's neck,
> And sucked divine ambrosia from her lips.   (II, i, 16–17)

The allusion alerts us to the intense beauty which may attend the
perverted and unnatural, and creates a parallel between the actions
of men and gods which ennobles and magnifies the incestuous love.
It is precisely at this point, when the human love is like to become
glorified, that Ford allows another voice to be heard. Putana's view
is not godlike:

> . . . and I say still, if a young wench feel the fit upon her, let her
> take anybody, father or brother, all is one.   (II, i, 44–5)

Taken seriously, this is to identify human life with animal life. As
Wayland Young points out:

> No animal which it has been possible to study (and this includes the
> apes) recognises its own kin once they are grown up. At a certain
> point, therefore, the human race must have learned to do this. Once
> we formed the concepts of sister, mother, daughter, brother, father
> and son, we were bound to distinguish, and endogamy and exogamy
> began.[9]

Yet Weinberg discovered that there are cases in contemporary society
in which an incestuous relationship is unaccompanied by guilt:

> If they didn't make so much to do about this whole mess, I'd go
> right back where I started from with my sister. We should have
> gone to some small town or some place where they didn't know us
> and we could live there like man and wife. . . . I don't regret at all
> that I had relations with my sister. (Case of Cu.)[10]

Putana's attitude represents a socially irresponsible, yet perfectly
real, attitude towards incest. But there is a difference between the
conceptual content of her attitude and its dramatic effect. At this
point in the play it comes as an almost cheerful reminder of the
coarse quality of ordinary life; the delicacy of the exchanges between

---

[9] Wayland Young, *Eros Denied*, 1965, p. 117.
[10] Weinberg, p. 156.

Giovanni and Annabella have almost spiritualised their passion into thin air, and Putana's intervention reminds us that incest is a matter of sex as well as love. Her function is not unlike that of Juliet's Nurse, counterpointing romantic love with stupid goodwill.

Giovanni and Annabella are not alone on stage again until V, v, at the climax of the play. They appear together with others, and they have their separate confessional scenes (II, v and III, vi), but the reticence of Ford's dramaturgy maintains a privacy about their love which dignifies it and affords it a tragic status. Indeed, in the whole exposition of the incestuous love theme the most powerful factor is the manifest objectivity of the dramatist himself. There is always a sense of an ordering mind behind the action, a creative consciousness which is concerned to mediate the events of the plot with an austere but subtle restraint. The topic may be sensational, but the treatment is not. Ford's is an art of ruthless realism.

The play's judgement on incestuous love is not passed until the Fifth Act, but the scene between the lovers is not a simple climax. The fifth and sixth scenes of Act V must be taken together as a complex judgement and a double resolution of the play's major theme. In the opening lines Giovanni, aware that their love has been betrayed, plays upon the concept of treachery in such a way as to divorce it completely from their present peril:

> . . . does the fit come on you, to prove treacherous
> To your past vows and oaths?   (V, v, 4–5)

The peril of discovery, disgrace and death is brushed aside:

> What danger's half so great as thy revolt?   (V, v, 8)

This is all for love, and the world of the spirit has precedence over the world of the flesh. Annabella is concerned with the immanence of death, but her words reveal that her concern is to establish a proper decorum for dying:

> This banquet is an harbinger of death
> To you and me; resolve yourself it is,
> And be prepared to welcome it.   (V, v, 27–9)

The talk drifts on to consideration of an after-life, and Annabella's orthodox religious affirmations balance Giovanni's lingering desires for the continuation of sexual love in the spiritual realm. The moral bearings shift, and the warmth of life and human love becomes momentarily important again. This sense of moral drift is part of the price exacted for incestuous love; they are cut away from the orthodox responses to concepts like Heaven and hell, rewards and punishments, and must live by the standards they forge for themselves. Once this point has been established—and Ford establishes it

with a deft economy in not more than a dozen lines—the world outside is permitted to assert its pressures again:

> . . . Some way think
> How to escape; I'm sure the guests are come.   (V, v, 43–4)

Action is forced upon them, and Giovanni assumes a rhetoric to
match the moment. What he says is of small importance compared
with the action and statement he is nerving himself to perform and
make. He asserts his love, and her beauty, persuades her to pray to a
God in whom he only casually believes, and pronounces that if after-
times know their full story they will not be too harshly judged. Then,
as he stabs her, and in answer to her question 'What means this?' he
gives his reasons:

> To save thy fame, and kill thee in a kiss.
> Thus die, and die by me, and by my hand.
> Revenge is mine; honour doth love command.   (V, v, 84–6)

Bowers, examining the play as an example of the revenge ethic, finds
it difficult to understand why Giovanni should call his deed a
revenge.[11] He notices that Giovanni describes it as such twice more,
in V, vi, when he answers his father's query about his sanity, and as
he stabs Soranzo. Bowers suggests that the explanation goes back to
Giovanni's words in I, i:

> All this I'll do, to free me from the rod
> Of vengeance; else I'll swear my fate's my god.   (I, i, 83–4)

He says: 'The inference is that on his failure God removes his
protection and Giovanni accordingly with desperate courage throws
himself for better or worse upon his fate. Buoyed up in this conviction with paranoiac hardihood, the normal functions of his mind
are gradually destroyed and he begins to feel that he can outface God
himself.' I cannot believe that, from an audience's point of view, the
concept of an over-arching fate, which takes over when God has
abandoned him, is sufficiently present in the play to explain
Giovanni's outburst satisfactorily. 'Fate', to him, is simply a word he
clings to at moments of high tension, and it is a word which has to do
with ideas of control and responsibility. We may paraphrase the
couplet which ends I, i, 'I'll do all you say, so that I can say I have
done all I can; but if that fails I'll make no further attempt to control my actions'. At the point where he has achieved the courage to
kill Annabella his moral vision is clouded, his control of language has
lapsed, his world is in pieces, 'all coherence gone'. This is madness,
and madness is the judgement upon him. In a sense, Annabella is

[11] F. T. Bowers, *Elizabethan Revenge Tragedy 1587–1642*, Princeton, 1940,
206–11.

dismissed more easily; her repentance and death, and the immaculate orthodoxy of her final prayer, open the prospect of a future life in which she will at least have opportunities for expiation. The dramatist's final attitude to her is one of pity. This is clear from the title of the play, which inevitably recalls Othello's 'Villain, be sure thou prove my love a whore', and later 'but yet the pity of it Iago! O Iago, the pity of it, Iago'. But Giovanni receives a sterner justice. His madness is brought about by the pressure of reconciling the orthodox meanings of concepts like 'honour', 'fame', 'revenge', 'justice' with the facts of his unique experience. In his situation there are no accepted meanings, no precedents, no controlling moral concepts. Even the word 'love' means something to him which no one else in the play can understand. He inhabits his own world of language, and that way madness lies.

The link between the object and the word signifying that object has been broken, and it is Ford's master-stroke that he found a dramatic correlative for the breakdown. When Giovanni enters 'with a heart upon his dagger' the metaphoric language in which the play has traded is suddenly dislocated. When he says:

> . . . 'tis a heart,
> A heart, my lords, in which is mine entombed:
> Look well upon't; d'ee know't?   (V, vi, 27–9)

the madness is obvious (you can't recognise a person by his heart), and yet, as dramatic metaphor, the symbol is completely viable. Love is brought on to the stage, on a dagger, dripping blood.

The judgement Ford makes on Giovanni is only possible in a social group where the brother/sister relationship is a central one. Ford was deeply interested in this relationship—he investigates it in four of his plays—and to this extent his society is unlike ours. The contemporary situation is described by an anthropologist, who wrote recently:

> With us, brother/sister relations are not formally structured. There is little to say about them anthropologically except the absence of attitudes which hold elsewhere. Why does the subject of brother/sister incest have so little interest for us while it occupies a great symbolic field of mythology and ritual in other parts of the world?[12]

The answer, she suggests, lies in the fact that 'the enduring formal structure of our society is based on rights to office and property, rights which are not gained by manipulation of kinship ties', and she concludes:

[12] Mary Douglas, in *New Society*, 15 June 1967, 872–3.

As the brother's role is more and more attenuated, the incest theme in Elizabethan drama . . . becomes more alien to us. It would be wrong to interpret the great mythologies of antiquity which depict the horror of brother/sister incest as merely enacting the emotions of childhood. The magnifying and glorifying social dimension gave the relation of brother to sister its special hold on the poetic imagination. For us the brother/sister theme has lost its poignancy as a great literary and dramatic symbol because the social tie has lost its central significance.

Ford's exploration and judgement of incestuous love should perhaps warn us not to assume too easily that our property-orientated morality is conducive to our cultural health.

OUT OF THE LOUD WORLD

Like *The Broken Heart*, *'Tis Pity* is, to some extent, a study in isolation. This is made clear in the very articulation of the opening scenes. After the rarified, intellectual yet passionate debate between the Friar and Giovanni in I, i, a dispute between master and pupil who have now become intellectual equals, we hear two new voices:

VASQUES
Come sir, stand to your tackling; if you prove craven, I'll make you run quickly.
GRIMALDI
Thou art no equal match for me.
VASQUES
Indeed I never went to the wars to bring home news, nor cannot play the mountebank for a meal's meat, and swear I got my wounds in the field. . . .   (I, ii, 1–6)

Social distinctions, status, rank, are loudly in question, and the quarrel introduces the world in which the strange love of Giovanni and Annabella is set. It is very much a 'domestic' world. Unlike Ford's other plays there are here no Kings, no princesses, no councils of state; it is a world of families, of citizens, merchants and physicians, and the highest places are occupied by Soranzo, a 'nobleman', and the Cardinal, nuncio to the Pope. The immediate effect of this is to insulate the developing love of Giovanni and Annabella from any concern with public affairs. Ford's play has sometimes been compared with *Antony and Cleopatra*,[13] but the essential difference between the two plays is that Shakespeare is concerned to demonstrate that where love is concerned kingdoms are clay, while Ford is careful to place as little as possible at hazard, to limit his world to the domestic and mercantile, to isolate his central theme.

[13] By T. S. Eliot, 'John Ford', in *Selected Essays*, 1951 edition, p. 197.

The quarrel between Vasques and Grimaldi brings a second group on stage, Florio, Donado and Soranzo, who immediately assert the proper 'citizen' reaction to riot. Florio talks of 'sudden broils', 'disordered bloods', 'unrest', and wants to be left 'to eat or sleep in peace at home', while Donado rebukes Vasques for 'seconding contentions'. Their protest is against anything which offers to disturb the peace and progress of their particular sector of society—a middle-class, bourgeois sector—and they represent the privileged, conservative element in the play's world. They are essentially upholders of the *status quo*, the stuff of which magistrates are made, concerned to explore nothing and to change nothing unless they have to. And, true to form, they arbitrate. 'What's the ground?', asks Florio, and they find themselves enmeshed in a contention about birth, and blood, and the right to woo. As they leave the stage to 'end this fray in wine' Putana, who with Annabella has overheard the account of the quarrel and the judgement, makes another of the play's 'isolating' statements:

> How like you this, child? Here's threatening, challenging, quarrelling, and fighting, on every side, and all is for your sake; you had need look to yourself, charge, you'll be stolen away sleeping else shortly. (I, ii, 63–6)

She asserts a world busy, bustling, active about the business of disposing of her 'charge'. The rhythms of Annabella's reply enforce a grave and detached simplicity of attitude which effectively insulates her from her surroundings:

> But, tut'ress, such a life gives no content
> To me, my thoughts are fixed on other ends;
> Would you would leave me. (I, ii, 67–9)

She withdraws almost into silence, while Putana prattles on about men and marriage, nobility and virility, until the entry of Bergetto and Poggio completes the chorus of the world's voices. Ford has justly been strictured for the inadequacy of his comic characters, and his attempts at comic situations are usually disastrous. Bergetto and Poggio are the exceptions. Ford succeeds with them because they are not simply clowns. Poggio is the undeceived yet loyal servant, while Bergetto, in his industrious stupidity, has an energy and a certain command of phrase ('I will but wash my face, and shift socks') which mark him off from Ford's other comic creations. He is concerned only for puppet-shows and wenches, and he stands at the opposite end of the social scale from his responsible uncle, Donado. The world of Parma displays all the vices and virtues associated with a mercantile society. Florio and Donado are deeply concerned with position, wealth, status, but Donado is equally concerned to further the interests of

his nephew Bergetto, using his skill, experience and influence to try
to make him acceptable to Annabella. Kindness, loyalty, generosity
can thrive in this society, which is, above all, a community of family
groups. And the greatest internal threat to a family group is the
possibility of incest.

Ford does not view the world of Parma in any sentimental light.
He concedes its energy and variety, but he has damning criticisms to
make of it. Grimaldi describes himself as 'a Roman and a gentleman;
one that have got mine honour with expense of blood', and Vasques
replies 'You are a lying coward and a fool'. Irving Ribner has pointed
out[14] that the meeting between Soranzo and Hippolita displays even
more clearly the rottenness on which this society's idea of honour
stands. Soranzo has seduced her with promises of marriage, he has
had a part in the assumed death of her husband, and now he rejects
her with a piece of hypocritical casuistry:

> The vows I made, if you remember well,
> Were wicked and unlawful: 'twere more sin
> To keep them than to break them.   (II, ii, 84–6)

The facts about his past are well known, and yet this is the man who
is generally accepted as the fittest claimant for Annabella's hand. It is
a world in which injustice can flourish. The Cardinal's protection of
Grimaldi after the murder of Bergetto is a flagrant misuse of power,
as is his final disposition of property at the end of the play:

> And all the gold and jewels, or whatsoever,
> Confiscate by the canons of the church,
> We seize upon to the Pope's proper use.   (V, vi, 149–51)

These are the values, and this is the morality of the church's repre-
sentative, and his are the values which triumph in the end.

The central acts of the play have comparatively little to do with
the main theme. Once the incest has been committed Giovanni and
Annabella retire from the scene, and the so-called 'sub-plot' assumes
control. Critics have been divided about the purpose of these central
scenes, some seeing them as disconnected and inchoate, while others
discover a unifying theme. Professor Bradbrook says:

> . . . in Ford's play there is no interconnection between the comic
> characters and the serious ones. Bergetto's wooing of Annabella is
> entirely without underlying purpose, and because the comedy is not
> used as comment on the tragedy, the lesser figures, such as Donado
> and Poggio, become mere supers.[15]

---

[14] Irving Ribner, *Jacobean Tragedy*, 1962, 169–70.
[15] M. C. Bradbrook, *Themes and Conventions of Elizabethan Tragedy*,
Cambridge, 1960 edition, p. 256.

Irving Ribner, on the other hand, argues

> The sub-plots are related to one another and controlled by the
> governing theme of the play in that each one is designed to make
> clear some aspect of the moral order which Giovanni cannot blindly
> accept.[16]

He goes on to show how the Cardinal, for example, is needed to pass
religion's judgement on Giovanni at the end of the play, while he is
himself displayed as corrupt and irreligious. While I do not myself
find the degree of schematisation that Ribner favours present in these
scenes, neither do they seem to me to be without an organising
principle. I would suggest that the centre of the play is concerned
with the attempt to bring Soranzo and Annabella together, and the
moral judgement which is passed on such a union in such a society.
In this way Ford opens a deep social perspective, showing how
Annabella, in particular, is knit so closely into her social background
that she can never break wholly free from it. Soranzo, as we have
seen, has transgressed the moral code, but in such a way that he has
not become an outcast from society. He stands, with all his imperfec-
tions on his head, as a nobleman and the most eligible suitor. But
Ford takes care to show how his sins have come home to roost.
Three out of the four minor actions in the plot are provided and
motivated by people seeking revenge against Soranzo: Grimaldi,
Hippolita and Richardetto. Grimaldi's reasons are as slight as his
own pretensions to honour; Hippolita is herself deeply flawed, and
implicated in the crime Soranzo is thought to have committed; only
Richardetto has genuinely been wronged by Soranzo, and has just
cause for seeking revenge.[17] Yet in Acts II and III the energies of all
these minor characters are devoted to the downfall of Soranzo. The
effect of this is to create a web of intrigue, with disguises and
'asides' and shifting of loyalties—in fact to submerge all honesty of
commerce between people, to set a gulf between a man's policy and
his profession. This is very much the way Ford sees society: material-
istic, affluent (there are no poor in Parma), acquisitive, bourgeois,
and with moral values to match. In such a society only the shrewd
and the rich survive. But this is not the whole picture. Just as
Soranzo is under attack from his would-be revengers, so Annabella
is under assault from the wooing of Bergetto. It is very much part of
her development towards a kind of self-sufficiency that she learns
how to control this threat to her integrity. In II, vi, when no amount
of polite evasion will suffice, she at last speaks out:

[16] Ribner, p. 164.
[17] It is worth noting that Richardetto is also the only character who gives up
the idea of revenge, unattempted.

Signor Donado, if your nephew mean
To raise his better fortunes in his match,
The hope of me will hinder such a hope;
Sir, if you love him, as I know you do,
Find one more worthy of his choice than me.
In short, I'm sure I sha' not be his wife.   (II, vi, 48–53)

This is plain dealing, and Donado applauds it as such, but it is also a
new tone in Annabella's voice, a blend of firmness with delicacy, the
achievement of a civilised decorum, a tone which she takes with her
into her conversations with Giovanni in Act V. The coming together
of Soranzo and Annabella in III, ii is a point of inner climax in the
play. It is aptly staged as an eavesdropping scene, since here the two
worlds, the public one of Soranzo and the private one of Giovanni,
come momentarily together. When Florio allows Soranzo 'private
speech' with Annabella they are left tactfully alone, until Giovanni
appears, unobserved, on the upper stage. It is an uneasy scene; there
is an underlying sense of *voyeurism* about it, a lack of trust and an
invasion of privacy. In many ways it is reminiscent of that much
more powerful scene in *Troilus and Cressida* (V, ii) in which
Cressida's faithlessness is observed by Troilus and Ulysses, and by
Thersites, so that the audience receives a double commentary on the
action. From one point of view the wooing of Soranzo and Annabella
is the confrontation between an adulterous attempted murderer and
an incest participant; from another it is the meeting of an eligible
nobleman with Signor Florio's daughter. Yet the audience is
presented with a third aspect: it is the spectacle of a tortured lover
watching another man offering love to his mistress. The complexity
of response which this scene arouses is the index of the depth of
Ford's vision into the society he anatomises. It is a typically busy,
pragmatic, slightly shabby society. And this isolates the unyielding
idealism of the two lovers, who stand outside its laws.

Una Ellis-Fermor puts this in another way when she says in a
perceptive footnote:

> In *'Tis Pity*, for instance, the central figures are sure and clear in
> mood; the confusion and obliquity lies in the vacillations of other
> characters such as the Friar and Richardetto.[18]

One may go further; the sureness and clarity of Giovanni and
Annabella is not simply a matter of mood, it extends to concepts and
arguments as well. If we compare the two scenes in which Giovanni
and Annabella respectively confront the Friar we see how their
'confessions' complement one another. In II, v Giovanni meets the
Friar's predictions of disaster with a set of arguments:

[18] Una Ellis-Fermor, *The Jacobean Drama*, fourth edition, with additions,
1961, pp. 244–5.

So where the body's furniture is beauty,
The mind's must needs be virtue; which allowed,
Virtue itself is reason but refined. . . .   (II, v, 18–20)

and so on. The arguments are not in themselves convincing (what arguments available to Giovanni would be?) but the dramatic effect is of a man totally in command of his situation, putting irresistible points. When, as the scene develops, we watch the Friar's arguments weakening, until he finally leaves logic and falls back on prayer, we are left aware that honest desire has triumphed over irresolute exhortation. In the corresponding scene with Annabella (III, vi) the Friar's approach is different. Annabella is discovered in a position of penitence, and the Friar offers to 'read a lecture'. He does so, at some length, and assumes that his words have borne fruit in repentance, but this is far from evident. Annabella's words are by no means conclusive: 'Wretched creature', 'Mercy, O mercy', 'Is there no way left to redeem my miseries?', 'Ay me'. She accedes to the Friar's suggestion that she should marry Soranzo, but the conversation at the betrothal shows that she has not yielded an inch in her moral stand:

FLORIO
Daughter, are you resolved?
ANNABELLA   Father, I am.
            Enter GIOVANNI, SORANZO, *and* VASQUES
FLORIO
My Lord Soranzo, here
Give me your hand; for that I give you this.
                                        [*Joins their hands*]
SORANZO
Lady, say you so too?
ANNABELLA   I do, and vow
To live with you and yours.   (III, vi, 50–4)

This is all she vows, and, as events turn out, all she performs. It has been suggested by critics who wished to extenuate Annabella's offence, that the liaison with Giovanni did not continue after her marriage. That it did continue is abundantly clear from the opening sixteen lines of V, iii, and this shows that whatever Annabella may have allowed herself to say under pressure her moral sense remains sure and clear. In the distinction between doing and being she is closely analogous to Penthea in *The Broken Heart*, who, when Ithocles asks her how her lord esteems her, replies:

                              Such an one
As only you have made me: a faith-breaker,
A spotted whore. Forgive me; I am one
In act, not in desires, the gods must witness.   (III, ii, 68–71)

Giovanni and Annabella, throughout the middle reaches of the play, pursue a straight, unwavering course. It is the world about them whose centre cannot hold.

In Ford's view this very integrity and persistence become in the end a sin. Annabella's defiance of Soranzo in IV, iii has that desperate quality which refuses to acknowledge his humanity:

> Let it suffice that you shall have the glory
> To father what so brave a father got.
> In brief, had not this chance fallen out as't doth,
> I never had been troubled with a thought
> That you had been a creature.   (IV, iii, 44–8)

Giovanni shows in his soliloquy in V, iii that he has reached a point where he is prepared to treat the rest of the world with contempt, because it is not worth his thought:

> Busy opinion is an idle fool,
> That, as a school-rod keeps a child in awe,
> Frights the unexperienced temper of the mind:
> So did it me . . .   (V, iii, 1–4)

> My world, and all of happiness, is here,
> And I'd not change it for the best to come:
> A life of pleasure is Elysium.   (V, iii, 14–16)

The lovers rate too highly the quality of their own experience, and in the end their experiences diverge. In the last Act Giovanni acts not *with* but *upon* his sister; his love has become selfish. As R. J. Kaufmann puts it:[19]

> Ford saw, and makes us see, that for Giovanni and for Annabella what has happened is a deeply working denial that others have a reality commensurate to the sense of their own being.

THE SOUND OF IT

Ford's images do not assert themselves. He has none of that virtuosity of language which is characteristic of so much Jacobean dramatic writing. His symbols are more commonly visual symbols, and especially 'spectacular' scenes. The death of Orgilus and the Dance scene in *The Broken Heart* are well known, though perhaps the most startling of these scenes in Ford is the appearance of Fernando in his winding sheet in the last Act of *Love's Sacrifice*. In

[19] R. J. Kaufmann, 'Ford's Tragic Perspective', *Texas Studies in Literature and Language* I (Winter 1960), pp. 522–37, and reprinted in *Elizabethan Drama: Modern Essays in Criticism*, ed. R. J. Kaufmann, New York and Oxford, 1961, 356–72.

'Tis Pity the entry of Giovanni with a heart on his dagger, in V, vi, is a scene of this kind—a visual, and essentially theatrical epitome of an aspect of the play. It functions on the stage almost like an emblem in a book, and it is significant to notice the way in which Ford has staged this particular revelation. Giovanni enters 'trimmed in reeking blood, That triumphs over death', and apart from the Cardinal's reaction 'What means this?' no one on stage says anything about the striking picture he presents. Giovanni is obliged to point out the fact that he has Annabella's heart in his hand, and still no one comments or moves. After some fifty lines Soranzo can still cry

> I shall burst with fury.
> Bring the strumpet forth.   (V, vi, 54–5)

and it is not until Vasques returns and confirms that Annabella is indeed dead that Giovanni's emblem is believed. And even then it is ignored. In theatrical terms this is marvellously right. The citizens of Parma have no idea how to react to a heart on a dagger, because it is no part of the world to which they belong. It is, however, the perfect, final, visual image for what has been going on privately, secretly, in their midst. Its aptness arises from its fulfilment of the symbolic scene with which the incestuous love began. When Giovanni and Annabella knelt, in I, ii, and vowed by their mother's dust not to betray each other their formulation was precise:

> Brother, even by our mother's dust, I charge you,
> Do not betray me to your mirth or hate,
> Love me, or kill me, brother.   (I, ii, 250–2)

This ritual promise is carried out, and seen to be carried out. Justice (from Giovanni's point of view) is plainly seen to be done, and the final spectacle is the completion of the prophecy.

The other 'spectacular' scene in *'Tis Pity* is of the same kind, and serves a similar purpose. Act IV opens with the banquet to celebrate the marriage of Soranzo and Annabella. The feasting is interrupted by the unexpected entry of Hippolita and Ladies in masks and white robes, with garlands of willow. The dance has all the appearance of a tribute to the occasion, and it is not until Hippolita unmasks that the truth is made known—she is a spectre at this particular feast. Both the feast and the dance represent an ordered ritual, the pattern of society, its safeguard and its peace. But the public action is not what it seems, and the equation between the false dance and the fake marriage enforces a moral point and brings together for a moment the hypocrisy of Hippolita and the hypocrisy of Annabella—the situation it offers for judgement is a complex one, and the scene does not last long enough for an audience to be obliged to take sides and apportion blame, but the claims of justice are brought to the fore, until they are overwhelmed by Hippolita's death.

'*Tis Pity* is an obsessive play (main plot and sub-plots are all concerned with marriage disasters), and the obsessive quality is reflected in the language. The play functions around a few key words which are repeated again and again until they achieve an almost hypnotic quality. The word 'blood', for example, occurs more than thirty times in the course of the play, and covers a fairly wide area of meaning:

> Cry to thy heart, wash every word thou utter'st
> In tears (and if 't be possible) of blood . . .   (I, i, 72–3)

> . . . a gentleman; one that have got mine honour with expense of
>   blood . . .   (II, i, 14–15)

> Have you not other places but my house
> To vent the spleen of your disordered bloods?   (II, i, 21–2)

> But know, Grimaldi, though, may be, thou art
> My equal in thy blood . . .   (II, i, 36–7)

> Her sickness is a fulness of her blood . . .   (III, iv, 8)

> The blood's yet seething hot, that will anon
> Be frozen harder than congealed coral . . .   (V, iii, 25–6)

All these, together with Bergetto's pathetic astonishment at the sight of his own blood, and Annabella's letter written in her blood, build up an insistence upon the word until the literal and metaphoric senses coalesce, and the word becomes almost co-extensive with life.[20] Ford plays upon the word 'heart' in the same way. There is a ground level of meaning, in which 'heart' is synonymous with 'feelings':

> Soranzo is the man that hath her heart . . .   (II, iii, 49)

> I need not now—my heart persuades me so— . . .   (IV, ii, 7)

which runs through the play, but there are also outcrops in which the word is used in a more literal sense, as a violent prolepsis of the spectacle in the final Act:

SORANZO
> Did you but see my heart, then you would swear—
ANNABELLA
> That you were dead.   (III, ii, 23–4)

[20] The same process can be seen taking place in D. H. Lawrence's *The Rainbow*; see especially the opening of chapter VIII.

SORANZO
    Not know it, strumpet? I'll rip up thy heart,
    And find it there.
ANNABELLA   Do, do!   (IV, iii, 53–4)

and once again there is a prophecy in the initial scene between
Giovanni and Annabella which is fatally fulfilled in the last. In I, ii
Giovanni offers his dagger to his sister, saying:

    And here's my breast, strike home.
    Rip up my bosom, there thou shalt behold
    A heart in which is writ the truth I speak.
    Why stand 'ee?   (I, ii, 205–8)

The word is used more than thirty-five times in the play, its senses
varying with its contexts, but always forcing together the literal and
the symbolic meanings, so that the repetition and the movement
together condition the reader or the audience for the visual fulfilment
of the last scene, when the word is made flesh. Donald K. Anderson
has examined both *'Tis Pity* and *The Broken Heart*[21] and established
close links between the 'heart' and 'banquet' images, but the
obsessive quality of the language seems much more powerful and
oppressive in *'Tis Pity* than in any of Ford's other plays. To take just
one more example, the unusual word 'confusion' rings through the
play, from Act IV to the end. Giovanni, faced with the fact of his
sister's marriage, says:

    Ere I'd endure this sight, to see my love
    Clipped by another, I would dare confusion,
    And stand the horror of ten thousand deaths.   (IV, i, 16–18)

Later in the same scene Vasques describes how Hippolita had
bribed him to poison Soranzo 'whiles she might laugh at his confusion on his marriage day'. In IV, ii Richardetto is confident of
Soranzo's immanent fall, and says:

    I need not now—my heart persuades me so—
    To further his confusion; there is One
    Above begins to work . . .   (IV, ii, 7–9)

The word takes on new resonance when Annabella uses it in V, i:

    But they who sleep in lethargies of lust   .
    Hug their confusion, making Heaven unjust . . . (V, i, 28–9)

and it is repeated by Giovanni in V, iii:

    Are we grown traitors to our own delights?
    Confusion take such dotage . . .   (V, iii, 38–9)

[21] Donald K. Anderson, Jr., 'The Heart and the Banquet: Imagery in Ford's
'Tis Pity She's a Whore and *The Broken Heart*', *Studies in English Literature
1500–1900*, II, 209–17.

But in what is one of the supremely beautiful and moving moments
in the play the word appears again, with such an overwhelming sense
of rightness that the other appearances might have been deliberate
preparations:

> Brother, dear brother, know what I have been,
> And know that now there's but a dining-time
> 'Twixt us and our confusion: (V, v, 16–18)

The word is crucially relevant to these lovers because they are walk-
ing in a world where they have no guide. In their exploration of their
love they have no conventions of behaviour or language to fall back
on, they have no access to the experience of others. Clarity and
sureness are vital to them; confusion, in all its senses, is their peril.

Yet despite this peculiar quality of language in the play there are
moments when Ford's unique voice is unmistakably heard. The
plain, still voice, at once simple and grave, cadenced, and wonder-
fully austere:

> ANNABELLA
> Comes this in sadness from you?
> GIOVANNI   Let some mischief
> Befall me soon, if I dissemble aught.
> ANNABELLA
> You are my brother Giovanni.
> GIOVANNI   You
> My sister Annabella; I know this . . .   (I, ii, 226–9)

It is present too in Annabella's soliloquy which opens Act V:

> Pleasures, farewell, and all ye thriftless minutes
> Wherein false joys have spun a weary life!
> To these my fortunes now I take my leave.
> Thou, precious Time, that swiftly rid'st in post
> Over the world, to finish up the race
> Of my last fate, here stay thy restless course,
> And bear to ages that are yet unborn
> A wretched, woeful woman's tragedy.   (V, i, 1–8)

In the last analysis it is this sensitive, searching, deliberate quality
of verse that guarantees Ford's essential seriousness. 'Tis Pity cannot be accused of being a play which uses the incest theme for
sensational effect. This charge might be brought against many of the
plays of the period, and, in our own day, it might be levelled at Mr
Osborne's *Under Plain Cover* with some truth, but Ford's idealistic
exploration of this peripheral state is trenchant and disturbing, but
it is never crude, never easy. 'Tis Pity displays the sin, and it offers no
alternative to it. Society is shown as corrupt, and incestuous love as a
relationship capable of deep and fragile beauty. It raises poignant social
questions for our age, and it may help us to exorcize them with truth.

NOTE ON THE TEXT

Q WAS printed by Nicholas Okes for Richard Collins and published in 1633. Although it was not entered on the Stationers' Register the fact that Ford provided a dedication is evidence that he authorised the publication, and the copy supplied to the printer seems to have been good. There are no clear indications that it was a playhouse copy; the stage-directions are full and detailed, but this is true of most of Ford's plays. He usually gave specific instructions on stage matters, and there would have been comparatively little for a prompter to do. The compositor of Q was frequently careless, misattributing speeches, duplicating words, and making occasional omissions, but the only real hiatus in the text occurs at IV, i, 85, where it seems likely that the MS. was illegible. Bawcutt suggests that there may have been a second compositor for gatherings H to K (from IV, iii, 15 onwards) since the mistakes in these gatherings tend to be of a different kind from those found earlier, and there are different habits in the use of italic type.

The text of this edition has been prepared from photostats of the Bodleian copy of Q (Malone 238(3)), collated against the British Museum copy, 1481 bb 18, but since Bawcutt's edition is based on a collation of sixteen copies in the British Isles I have paid great attention to his text, and recorded all the press-variants he prints. In the matter of the distribution of prose and verse, in which Q is often unreliable, there is a considerable measure of agreement amongst editors. I have followed Bawcutt's decisions, with the single exception of II, i, 33–4.

FURTHER READING

THE FOLLOWING works may be useful in pursuing some of the ideas in the Introduction and Notes:

Anderson, Donald K. 'The Heart and Banquet: Imagery in Ford's *'Tis Pity She's a Whore* and *The Broken Heart*', *Studies in English Literature 1500–1900*, II, 209–17.

Comfort, A. *Sexual Behaviour in Society*, New York, 1950.

Freud, Sigmund. *Totem and Taboo*, trans. Strachey, 1950.

Lukacs, Georg. *The Meaning of Contemporary Realism*, trans. J. and N. Mander, 1963.

Osborne, John. *Under Plain Cover*, in *Plays for England*, 1963.

Sloane & Karpinski, 'Effects of Incest Upon the Participants', *American Journal of Orthopsychiatry*, xii (1942), 656–74.

Weinberg, S. K. *Incest Behavior*, New York, 1955.

Young, Wayland. *Eros Denied*, 1965.

Other critical accounts of the play, and of Ford's work in general, are as follows:

Davril, R. *Le Drame de John Ford*, Paris, 1954.

Eliot, T. S. 'John Ford', in *Selected Essays*, 1951 edition, 193–204.

Ellis-Fermor, U. M. *The Jacobean Drama*, revised edition, 1958.

Ewing, B. S. *Burtonian Melancholy in the Plays of John Ford*, Princeton, 1940.

Kaufmann, R. J. 'Ford's Tragic Perspective', *Texas Studies in Literature and Language*, I (Winter 1960), 522–37, and reprinted in *Elizabethan Drama: Modern Essays in Criticism*, ed. R. J. Kaufmann, New York and Oxford, 1961, 356–72.

Leech, C. *John Ford and the Drama of his Time*, 1957.

Oliver, H. J. *The Problem of John Ford*, Melbourne, 1955.

Ribner, Irving. *Jacobean Tragedy*, 1962.

Sargeaunt, M. J. *John Ford*, Oxford, 1935.

Sensebaugh, G. F. *The Tragic Muse of John Ford*, Stanford and London, 1944.

Stavig, Mark. *John Ford and the Traditional Moral Order*, Madison and London, 1968.

Tomlinson, T. B. *A Study of Elizabethan and Jacobean Tragedy*, Cambridge and Parkville (Vic.), 1969.

'TIS
Pitty Shee s a Whore

Acted by the *Queenes* Maiesties Seruants, at *The Phænix in
Drury-Lane.*

LONDON.
Printed by *Nicholas Okes* for *Richard
Collins,* and are to be sold at his shop
in *Pauls* Church-yard, at the signe
of the three Kings. 1633.

TO MY FRIEND THE AUTHOR

With admiration I beheld this Whore
Adorned with beauty such as might restore
(If ever being as thy muse hath famed)
Her Giovanni, in his love unblamed:
The ready Graces lent their willing aid,
Pallas herself now played the chambermaid,
And helped to put her dressings on. Secure
Rest thou that thy name herein shall endure
To th' end of age; and Annabella be
Gloriously fair, even in her infamy.

THOMAS ELLICE

Thomas Ellice. Nothing is known of him, but it seems likely that he was related to Robert Ellice of Gray's Inn, to whom Ford dedicated *The Lover's Melancholy*. The leaf on which the above lines appear is missing from many copies of Q.

TO THE TRULY NOBLE
JOHN, EARL OF PETERBOROUGH, LORD
MORDAUNT, BARON OF TURVEY

MY LORD,

Where a truth of merit hath a general warrant, there love is but a debt, acknowledgment a justice. Greatness cannot often claim virtue by inheritance; yet in this, yours appears most eminent, for that you are not more rightly heir to your fortunes than glory shall be to your memory. Sweetness of disposition   5
ennobles a freedom of birth; in both, your lawful interest adds honour to your own name and mercy to my presumption. Your noble allowance of these first fruits of my leisure in the action emboldens my confidence of your as noble construction in this presentment; especially since my service must ever owe   10
particular duty to your favours by a particular engagement. The gravity of the subject may easily excuse the lightness of the title, otherwise I had been a severe judge against mine own guilt. Princes have vouchsafed grace to trifles offered from a purity of devotion; your lordship may likewise please to admit   15
into your good opinion, with these weak endeavours, the constancy of affection from the sincere lover of your deserts in honour,

JOHN FORD

8 *allowance* approval
8–9 *in the action* on stage
9 *construction* interpretation
10 *in this presentment* in print

John Mordaunt (1599–1642) had been a courtier since boyhood, when James I was struck with his intelligence and beauty. He was created first Earl of Peterborough on 9 March 1627/8 by Charles I. On the outbreak of the civil war he adhered to Parliament and was general of ordnance under the Earl of Essex, but died of consumption on 18 June 1642. Nothing is known about the relationship between playwright and patron.

The Actors' Names

BONAVENTURA, a friar.
A CARDINAL, nuncio to the Pope.
SORANZO, a nobleman.
FLORIO, a citizen of Parma.
DONADO, another citizen.
GRIMALDI, a Roman gentleman.
GIOVANNI, son to Florio.
BERGETTO, nephew to Donado.
RICHARDETTO, a supposed physician.
VASQUES, servant to Soranzo.
POGGIO, servant to Bergetto.
BANDITTI, [OFFICERS, SERVANTS etc.].

Women

ANNABELLA, daughter to Florio.
HIPPOLITA, wife to Richardetto.
PHILOTIS, his niece.
PUTANA, tut'ress to Annabella.

The Scene:
PARMA

'TIS PITY SHE'S A WHORE

[Act I, Scene i]

Enter FRIAR *and* GIOVANNI

FRIAR
Dispute no more in this, for know, young man,
These are no school-points; nice philosophy
May tolerate unlikely arguments,
But Heaven admits no jest: wits that presumed
On wit too much, by striving how to prove   5
There was no God, with foolish grounds of art,
Discovered first the nearest way to hell,
And filled the world with devilish atheism.
Such questions, youth, are fond; for better 'tis
To bless the sun than reason why it shines;   10
Yet He thou talk'st of is above the sun.
No more; I may not hear it.
GIOVANNI   Gentle father,
To you I have unclasped my burdened soul,
Emptied the storehouse of my thoughts and heart,
Made myself poor of secrets; have not left   15
Another word untold, which hath not spoke
All what I ever durst, or think, or know;
And yet is here the comfort I shall have,
Must I not do what all men else may, love?
FRIAR
Yes, you may love, fair son.
GIOVANNI   Must I not praise   20
That beauty which, if framed anew, the gods
Would make a god of, if they had it there,
And kneel to it, as I do kneel to them?
FRIAR
Why, foolish madman!

---

2 *school-points* matters for academic discussion or debate
6 *art* knowledge
9 *fond* foolish

This scene is very similar in dramatic function and tone to the scene
between Orgilus and Tecnicus in *The Broken Heart*, I.iii, 1–32.

GIOVANNI   Shall a peevish sound,
  A customary form, from man to man,   25
  Of brother and of sister, be a bar
  'Twixt my perpetual happiness and me?
  Say that we had one father, say one womb
  (Curse to my joys) gave both us life and birth;
  Are we not therefore each to other bound   30
  So much the more by nature? by the links
  Of blood, of reason? nay, if you will have't,
  Even of religion, to be ever one,
  One soul, one flesh, one love, one heart, one all?
FRIAR
  Have done, unhappy youth, for thou art lost.   35
GIOVANNI
  Shall then, for that I am her brother born,
  My joys be ever banished from her bed?
  No, father; in your eyes I see the change
  Of pity and compassion; from your age,
  As from a sacred oracle, distils   40
  The life of counsel: tell me, holy man,
  What cure shall give me ease in these extremes.
FRIAR
  Repentance, son, and sorrow for this sin:
  For thou hast moved a Majesty above
  With thy unranged (almost) blasphemy.   45
GIOVANNI
  O do not speak of that, dear confessor.
FRIAR
  Art thou, my son, that miracle of wit
  Who once, within these three months, wert esteemed
  A wonder of thine age, throughout Bononia?
  How did the University applaud   50
  Thy government, behaviour, learning, speech,
  Sweetness, and all that could make up a man!

24 *peevish* trifling (see V.iii, 40)
25 *customary form* conventional formality
45 *unranged* disordered, deranged
46 *confessor* accented on first syllable
49 *Bononia* Bologna, famous for its university
51 *government* way of life

28–34 *Say that . . . all.* Cf. Giovanni's use of the same argument at I.ii, 235ff.

I was proud of my tutelage, and chose
Rather to leave my books than part with thee.
I did so: but the fruits of all my hopes   55
Are lost in thee, as thou art in thyself.
O, Giovanni, hast thou left the schools
Of knowledge to converse with lust and death?
For death waits on thy lust. Look through the world,
And thou shalt see a thousand faces shine   60
More glorious than this idol thou ador'st:
Leave her, and take thy choice, 'tis much less sin,
Though in such games as those they lose that win.

GIOVANNI
It were more ease to stop the ocean
From floats and ebbs than to dissuade my vows.   65

FRIAR
Then I have done, and in thy wilful flames
Already see thy ruin; Heaven is just.
Yet hear my counsel.

GIOVANNI   As a voice of life.

FRIAR
Hie to thy father's house, there lock thee fast
Alone within thy chamber, then fall down   70
On both thy knees, and grovel on the ground:
Cry to thy heart, wash every word thou utter'st
In tears (and if't be possible) of blood:

---

57 *Giovanni* four syllables
65 *vows* wishes, prayers (Latin *vota*)

53–4 *I was . . . thee.* Despite its European reputation throughout the
   Middle Ages the University of Bologna does not seem to have had any
   fixed residence before 1562. Until then professors lectured in their own
   houses, or later in rooms hired or lent by the civic authorities.

62 *'tis much less sin.* The view that fornication is a lesser sin than incest is
   probably based on the argument exemplified by Montaigne, *Of Modera-
   tion* (Florio's translation, 1603): 'The love we beare to women is very
   lawful; yet doth Divinitie bridle and restraine the same. I remember to
   have read in Saint Thomas, in a place where he condemneth marriages
   of kinsfolkes in forbidden degrees, this one reason amongst others; that
   the love a man beareth to such a woman may be immoderate; for, if the
   wedlocke, or husband-like affection be sound and perfect, as it ought to
   be, and also surcharged with that a man oweth to alliance and kindred;
   there is no doubt but that surcease may easily transport a husband
   beyond the bounds of reason.'

65 *floats.* The flux or flood of a tide. Cf. *Love's Sacrifice*, II.iii, 'though the
   float/of infinite desires swell to a tide/Too high so soon to ebb . . .'

Beg Heaven to cleanse the leprosy of lust
That rots thy soul, acknowledge what thou art,   75
A wretch, a worm, a nothing: weep, sigh, pray
Three times a day, and three times every night.
For seven days' space do this, then if thou find'st
No change in thy desires, return to me:
I'll think on remedy. Pray for thyself   80
At home, whilst I pray for thee here.—Away,
My blessing with thee, we have need to pray.

GIOVANNI
All this I'll do, to free me from the rod
Of vengeance; else I'll swear my fate's my god.   *Exeunt*

[Act I, Scene ii]

Enter GRIMALDI *and* VASQUES *ready to fight*

VASQUES
Come sir, stand to your tackling; if you prove craven, I'll
make you run quickly.

GRIMALDI
Thou art no equal match for me.

VASQUES
Indeed I never went to the wars to bring home news, nor
cannot play the mountebank for a meal's meat, and swear   5
I got my wounds in the field. See you these grey hairs?
They'll not flinch for a bloody nose. Wilt thou to this gear?

GRIMALDI
Why, slave, think'st thou I'll balance my reputation with
a cast-suit? Call thy master, he shall know that I dare—

VASQUES
Scold like a cot-quean, that's your profession. Thou poor   10
shadow of a soldier, I will make thee know my master keeps
servants thy betters in quality and performance. Com'st thou
to fight or prate?

1 *tackling* weapons
7 *gear* business (i.e. of fighting)
9 *cast-suit* dependent (wearing his master's old clothes)
10 *cot-quean* shrew, vulgar woman (*O.E.D.* 2)

84 *my fate's my god.* This is the first of Giovanni's references to being
  governed by destiny. The progress of this fatalism can be traced, with
  its various modulations, through the play: see I.ii, 139, I.ii, 224–5,
  III.ii, 20, V.v, 11–12, V.vi, 11, 72.

GRIMALDI

  Neither, with thee. I am a Roman and a gentleman; one that
  have got mine honour with expense of blood.   15

VASQUES

  You are a lying coward and a fool. Fight, or by these hilts
  I'll kill thee—brave my lord!—you'll fight?

GRIMALDI

  Provoke me not, for if thou dost—

VASQUES

  Have at you!   *They fight;* GRIMALDI *hath the worst*

Enter FLORIO, DONADO, SORANZO

FLORIO

  What mean these sudden broils so near my doors?   20
  Have you not other places but my house
  To vent the spleen of your disordered bloods?
  Must I be haunted still with such unrest
  As not to eat or sleep in peace at home?
  Is this your love, Grimaldi? Fie, 'tis naught.   25

DONADO

  And Vasques, I may tell thee 'tis not well
  To broach these quarrels; you are ever forward
  In seconding contentions.

Enter above ANNABELLA *and* PUTANA

FLORIO   What's the ground?

SORANZO

  That, with your patience, signors, I'll resolve:
  This gentleman, whom fame reports a soldier,   30
  (For else I know not) rivals me in love
  To Signor Florio's daughter, to whose ears
  He still prefers his suit, to my disgrace,
  Thinking the way to recommend himself
  Is to disparage me in his report.   35
  But know, Grimaldi, though, may be, thou art
  My equal in thy blood, yet this bewrays
  A lowness in thy mind which, wert thou noble,

20 *mean* Q *a.c.*; meaned Q *b.c.*
37 *bewrays* reveals

---

28 s.d. *Enter above.* i.e. on the upper stage, in order to hear the ensuing
    dialogue unobserved. They then overhear Bergetto and Poggio (103–
    16), and when Giovanni enters below they descend from the upper to
    the main stage during his soliloquy (139–58). Some editors un-
    necessarily begin a new scene after line 138.

Thou wouldst as much disdain as I do thee
For this unworthiness; and on this ground   40
I willed my servant to correct his tongue,
Holding a man so base no match for me.

VASQUES

And had not your sudden coming prevented us, I had let my
gentleman blood under the gills; I should have wormed
you, sir, for running mad.   45

GRIMALDI

I'll be revenged, Soranzo.

VASQUES

On a dish of warm broth to stay your stomach—do, honest
innocence, do; spoon-meat is a wholesomer diet than a
Spanish blade.

GRIMALDI

Remember this.   50

SORANZO

I fear thee not, Grimaldi.   *Exit* GRIMALDI

FLORIO

My Lord Soranzo, this is strange to me,
Why you should storm, having my word engaged:
Owing her heart, what need you doubt her ear?
Losers may talk by law of any game.   55

VASQUES

Yet the villainy of words, Signor Florio, may be such as
would make any unspleened dove choleric. Blame not my
lord in this.

FLORIO

Be you more silent.
I would not for my wealth my daughter's love   60

41 *his* ed. this Q
43 *had not* ed. had Q
45 *for* to prevent
48 *innocence* fool
54 *Owing* Owning
56 *villainy* ed. villaine Q

---

44 *wormed.* The small vermiform ligament in a dog's tongue was often cut
out in puppyhood, as a supposed safeguard against rabies. Vasques'
anger moves easily from fish (line 44) to dog.

57 *unspleened dove.* The idea that the dove has no gall is an ancient fallacy.
It is discussed and rejected by Sir Thomas Browne, *Pseudodoxia
Epidemica,* III.iii, though he allows a metaphoric sense: 'If therefore
any affirm a Pigeon hath no gall, implying no more thereby then the
lenity of the Animal, we shall not controvert his affirmation.'

Should cause the spilling of one drop of blood.
Vasques, put up, let's end this fray in wine.

        Exeunt [FLORIO, DONADO, SORANZO *and* VASQUES]

PUTANA

How like you this, child? Here's threatening, challenging,
quarrelling, and fighting, on every side, and all is for your
sake; you had need look to yourself, charge, you'll be stolen   65
away sleeping else shortly.

ANNABELLA

But, tut'ress, such a life gives no content
To me, my thoughts are fixed on other ends;
Would you would leave me.

PUTANA

Leave you? No marvel else. Leave me no leaving, charge;   70
this is love outright. Indeed I blame you not, you have choice
fit for the best lady in Italy.

ANNABELLA

Pray do not talk so much.

PUTANA

Take the worst with the best, there's Grimaldi the soldier,
a very well-timbered fellow. They say he is a Roman,   75
nephew to the Duke Montferrato, they say he did good
service in the wars against the Milanese, but 'faith, charge,
I do not like him, an't be for nothing but for being a soldier;
not one amongst twenty of your skirmishing captains but
have some privy maim or other that mars their standing   80
upright. I like him the worse, he crinkles so much in the
hams; though he might serve if there were no more men,
yet he's not the man I would choose.

ANNABELLA

Fie, how thou prat'st.

PUTANA

As I am a very woman, I like Signor Soranzo well; he is   85
wise, and what is more, rich; and what is more than that,
kind, and what is more than all this, a nobleman; such a
one, were I the fair Annabella myself, I would wish and
pray for. Then he is bountiful; besides, he is handsome, and
by my troth, I think wholesome (and that's news in a gallant   90
of three and twenty); liberal, that I know; loving, that you

62 *put up* sheathe your sword
78 *an't* ed. and Q
79 *not one* ed. one Q
80-1 *mars . . . upright* makes them impotent
90 *wholesome* not diseased

know; and a man sure, else he could never ha' purchased
such a good name with Hippolita, the lusty widow, in her
husband's lifetime: and 'twere but for that report, sweetheart, would 'a were thine. Commend a man for his qualities,   95
but take a husband as he is a plain-sufficient, naked man:
such a one is for your bed, and such a one is Signor Soranzo,
my life for't.

ANNABELLA
Sure the woman took her morning's draught too soon.

Enter BERGETTO *and* POGGIO

PUTANA
But look, sweetheart, look what thing comes now: here's   100
another of your ciphers to fill up the number. O brave old
ape in a silken coat. Observe.

BERGETTO
Didst thou think, Poggio, that I would spoil my new clothes,
and leave my dinner, to fight?

POGGIO
No, sir, I did not take you for so arrant a baby.   105

BERGETTO
I am wiser than so: for I hope, Poggio, thou never heardst
of an elder brother that was a coxcomb. Didst, Poggio?

POGGIO
Never indeed, sir, as long as they had either land or money
left them to inherit.

BERGETTO
Is it possible, Poggio? O monstrous! Why, I'll undertake   110
with a handful of silver to buy a headful of wit at any time;
but sirrah, I have another purchase in hand, I shall have the
wench, mine uncle says. I will but wash my face, and shift
socks, and then have at her i'faith. Mark my pace, Poggio.

POGGIO
Sir—[*Aside*] I have seen an ass and a mule trot the Spanish   115
pavin with a better grace, I know not how often.

Exeunt [BERGETTO *and* POGGIO]

ANNABELLA
This idiot haunts me too.

PUTANA
Ay, ay, he needs no description; the rich magnifico that is

116 *pavin* pavan, a grave, stately dance

101–2 *O brave old ape* etc. Proverbial: An ape is an ape though clad in
    scarlet (Tilley, A263).

below with your father, charge, Signor Donado his uncle,
for that he means to make this his cousin a golden calf,   120
thinks that you will be a right Israelite and fall down to him
presently: but I hope I have tutored you better. They say a
fool's bauble is a lady's playfellow, yet you having wealth
enough, you need not cast upon the dearth of flesh at any
rate: hang him, innocent.   125

Enter GIOVANNI

ANNABELLA
But see, Putana, see: what blessed shape
Of some celestial creature now appears?
What man is he, that with such sad aspect
Walks careless of himself?
PUTANA   Where?
ANNABELLA   Look below.
PUTANA
O, 'tis your brother, sweet.
ANNABELLA   Ha!
PUTANA   'Tis your brother.   130
ANNABELLA
Sure 'tis not he; this is some woeful thing
Wrapped up in grief, some shadow of a man.
Alas, he beats his breast, and wipes his eyes
Drowned all in tears: methinks I hear him sigh.
Let's down, Putana, and partake the cause;   135
I know my brother, in the love he bears me,
Will not deny me partage in his sadness.
My soul is full of heaviness and fear.   *Exit [with* PUTANA]
GIOVANNI
Lost. I am lost. My fates have doomed my death.
The more I strive, I love; the more I love,   140
The less I hope: I see my ruin, certain.
What judgment or endeavours could apply
To my incurable and restless wounds
I throughly have examined, but in vain.

120 *cousin* kinsman, here nephew
120 *golden calf* see Exodus, 32
123 *bauble* baton or stick (with an indecent pun)
137 *partage* a part or share
144 *throughly* thoroughly

123–5 *yet you . . . rate.* i.e. you are rich enough; you need not wager
recklessly and accept Bergetto for fear you will have no other suitors.

O that it were not in religion sin   145
To make our love a god, and worship it.
I have even wearied Heaven with prayers, dried up
The spring of my continual tears, even starved
My veins with daily fasts: what wit or art
Could counsel, I have practised; but alas,   150
I find all these but dreams and old men's tales
To fright unsteady youth; I'm still the same.
Or I must speak, or burst. 'Tis not, I know,
My lust, but 'tis my fate that leads me on.
Keep fear and low faint-hearted shame with slaves;   155
I'll tell her that I love her, though my heart
Were rated at the price of that attempt.
O me! She comes.

Enter ANNABELLA *and* PUTANA

ANNABELLA   Brother.
GIOVANNI [*Aside*]   If such a thing
As courage dwell in men, ye heavenly powers,
Now double all that virtue in my tongue.   160
ANNABELLA
Why, brother, will you not speak to me?
GIOVANNI
Yes; how d'ee, sister?
ANNABELLA
Howsoever I am, methinks you are not well.
PUTANA
Bless us, why are you so sad, sir?
GIOVANNI
Let me entreat you, leave us a while, Putana. Sister,   165
I would be private with you.
ANNABELLA
Withdraw, Putana.
PUTANA
I will. [*Aside*] If this were any other company for her, I

155 *Keep fear* Let fear dwell

145–6 *sin To make our love a god.* This is precisely Adam's sin in Paradise:
                . . . he scrupl'd not to eat
                Against his better knowledge, not deceav'd,
                But fondly overcome with Femal charm.
                            (*Paradise Lost*, IX, 997–9)
    Adam sinned deliberately, preferring the love of Eve to the love of
God, as St Paul recognises (1 Timothy 2. 14).

should think my absence an office of some credit; but I
will leave them together.   *Exit* PUTANA 170

GIOVANNI
Come, sister, lend your hand, let's walk together.
I hope you need not blush to walk with me;
Here's none but you and I.

ANNABELLA
How's this?

GIOVANNI
Faith, I mean no harm.   175

ANNABELLA
Harm?

GIOVANNI
No, good faith; how is't with 'ee?

ANNABELLA
[*Aside*] I trust he be not frantic.—I am very well, brother.

GIOVANNI
Trust me, but I am sick, I fear so sick
'Twill cost my life.   180

ANNABELLA
Mercy forbid it. 'Tis not so, I hope.

GIOVANNI
I think you love me, sister.

ANNABELLA
Yes, you know I do.

GIOVANNI
I know't indeed.—Y'are very fair.

ANNABELLA
Nay then, I see you have a merry sickness.   185

GIOVANNI
That's as it proves. The poets feign, I read,
That Juno for her forehead did exceed
All other goddesses: but I durst swear
Your forehead exceeds hers, as hers did theirs.

ANNABELLA
Troth, this is pretty.

169 *of some credit* deserving reward
186 *The* ed. They Q

187-8 *That Juno . . . goddesses.* Apart from her beauty, Juno is an apt
    choice for Giovanni to make at this point, since she was not only the
    wife of Jupiter, but his sister as well. See Ovid, *Fasti*, 6, 29, and
    Homer, *Iliad*, xvi.

GIOVANNI   Such a pair of stars   190
  As are thine eyes would, like Promethean fire,
  If gently glanced, give life to senseless stones.
ANNABELLA
  Fie upon 'ee.
GIOVANNI
  The lily and the rose, most sweetly strange,
  Upon your dimpled cheeks do strive for change.   195
  Such lips would tempt a saint; such hands as those
  Would make an anchorite lascivious.
ANNABELLA
  D'ee mock me, or flatter me?
GIOVANNI
  If you would see a beauty more exact
  Than art can counterfeit or nature frame,   200
  Look in your glass and there behold your own.
ANNABELLA
  O you are a trim youth.
GIOVANNI
  Here.   *Offers his dagger to her*
ANNABELLA
  What to do?
GIOVANNI
  And here's my breast, strike home.   205
  Rip up my bosom, there thou shalt behold
  A heart in which is writ the truth I speak.
  Why stand 'ee?
ANNABELLA   Are you earnest?
GIOVANNI   Yes, most earnest.
  You cannot love?
ANNABELLA   Whom?
GIOVANNI   Me. My tortured soul
  Hath felt affliction in the heat of death.   210
  O Annabella, I am quite undone.
  The love of thee, my sister, and the view
  Of thy immortal beauty hath untuned
  All harmony both of my rest and life.
  Why d'ee not strike?

205 *strike* ed. strick Q

191–2 *Promethean . . . stones.* One of Ford's typically suggestive phrases,
    recalling both *Othello*, V.ii, 12 'I know not where is that Promethean
    heat', and Chapman's *Bussy D'Ambois*, V.iii, 191–2 'like a falling star
    Silently glanc'd.'

ANNABELLA   Forbid it, my just fears.   215
  If this be true, 'twere fitter I were dead.
GIOVANNI
  True, Annabella; 'tis no time to jest.
  I have too long suppressed the hidden flames
  That almost have consumed me; I have spent
  Many a silent night in sighs and groans,   220
  Ran over all my thoughts, despised my fate,
  Reasoned against the reasons of my love,
  Done all that smoothed-cheek virtue could advise,
  But found all bootless: 'tis my destiny
  That you must either love, or I must die.   225
ANNABELLA
  Comes this in sadness from you?
GIOVANNI   Let some mischief
  Befall me soon, if I dissemble aught.
ANNABELLA
  You are my brother Giovanni.
GIOVANNI   You
  My sister Annabella; I know this:
  And could afford you instance why to love   230
  So much the more for this; to which intent
  Wise nature first in your creation meant
  To make you mine; else't had been sin and foul
  To share one beauty to a double soul.
  Nearness in birth or blood doth but persuade   235
  A nearer nearness in affection.
  I have asked counsel of the holy church,
  Who tells me I may love you, and 'tis just
  That since I may, I should; and will, yes, will.
  Must I now live, or die?
ANNABELLA   Live. Thou hast won   240
  The field, and never fought; what thou hast urged
  My captive heart had long ago resolved.
  I blush to tell thee—but I'll tell thee now—
  For every sigh that thou hast spent for me
  I have sighed ten; for every tear shed twenty: 245
  And not so much for that I loved, as that
  I durst not say I loved, nor scarcely think it.

224 *bootless* useless
226 *sadness* earnest   246 *for that* because

232–4 *Wise nature . . . soul.* Cf. Spenser, *An Hymne in Honour of Beautie*,
  204–10.

GIOVANNI
  Let not this music be a dream, ye gods,
  For pity's sake, I beg 'ee.
ANNABELLA   On my knees,   *She kneels*
  Brother, even by our mother's dust, I charge you,   250
  Do not betray me to your mirth or hate,
  Love me, or kill me, brother.
GIOVANNI   On my knees,   *He kneels*
  Sister, even by my mother's dust, I charge you,
  Do not betray me to your mirth or hate,
  Love me, or kill me, sister.   255
ANNABELLA
  You mean good sooth then?
GIOVANNI   In good troth I do,
  And so do you, I hope: say, I'm in earnest.
ANNABELLA
  I'll swear't, I.
GIOVANNI   And I, and by this kiss,   *Kisses her*
  (Once more, yet once more; now let's rise by this)
                                        [*They rise*]
  I would not change this minute for Elysium.   260
  What must we now do?
ANNABELLA   What you will.
GIOVANNI   Come then,
  After so many tears as we have wept,
  Let's learn to court in smiles, to kiss, and sleep.   *Exeunt*

[Act I, Scene iii]

Enter FLORIO *and* DONADO

FLORIO
  Signor Donado, you have said enough,
  I understand you; but would have you know
  I will not force my daughter 'gainst her will.
  You see I have but two, a son and her;
  And he is so devoted to his book,   5
  As I must tell you true, I doubt his health:
  Should he miscarry, all my hopes rely
  Upon my girl; as for worldly fortune,
  I am, I thank my stars, blest with enough.

256 *sooth* truth
258 *swear't, I* ed. swear't and I Q
  6 *doubt* fear for
  8 *girl* pronounced as two syllables throughout

My care is how to match her to her liking: 10
I would not have her marry wealth, but love,
And if she like your nephew, let him have her.
Here's all that I can say.

DONADO   Sir, you say well,
Like a true father, and for my part I,
If the young folks can like ('twixt you and me),   15
Will promise to assure my nephew presently
Three thousand florins yearly during life,
And after I am dead, my whole estate.

FLORIO
'Tis a fair proffer, sir; meantime your nephew
Shall have free passage to commence his suit.   20
If he can thrive, he shall have my consent.
So for this time I'll leave you, signor.   *Exit*

DONADO   Well,
Here's hope yet, if my nephew would have wit;
But he is such another dunce, I fear
He'll never win the wench. When I was young   25
I could have done't, i'faith, and so shall he
If he will learn of me; and in good time
He comes himself.

Enter BERGETTO *and* POGGIO

How now, Bergetto, whither away so fast?

BERGETTO
O uncle, I have heard the strangest news that ever came   30
out of the mint, have I not, Poggio?

POGGIO
Yes indeed, sir.

DONADO
What news, Bergetto?

BERGETTO
Why, look ye, uncle, my barber told me just now that
there is a fellow come to town who undertakes to make a   35
mill go without the mortal help of any water or wind, only
with sand-bags: and this fellow hath a strange horse, a most
excellent beast, I'll assure you, uncle (my barber says),

29 *How . . . fast* Assigned to Donado since Weber's edition (1811);
     to Poggio in Q

30–1 *that ever came out of the mint.* Proverbial: New out of the Mint
     (Tilley M985). Cf. *Twelfth Night*, III.ii, 22 '. . . some excellent jests,
     fire-new from the mint.'

whose head, to the wonder of all Christian people, stands
just behind where his tail is. Is't not true, Poggio?   40

POGGIO

So the barber swore, forsooth.

DONADO

And you are running thither?

BERGETTO

Ay forsooth, uncle.

DONADO

Wilt thou be a fool still? Come sir, you shall not go: you
have more mind of a puppet-play than on the business I   45
told ye; why, thou great baby, wilt never have wit, wilt
make thyself a may-game to all the world?

POGGIO

Answer for yourself, master.

BERGETTO

Why, uncle, should I sit at home still, and not go abroad to
see fashions like other gallants?   50

DONADO

To see hobby-horses! What wise talk, I pray, had you with
Annabella, when you were at Signor Florio's house?

BERGETTO

O, the wench! Uds sa' me, uncle, I tickled her with a rare
speech, that I made her almost burst her belly with laughing.

DONADO

Nay, I think so; and what speech was't?   55

BERGETTO

What did I say, Poggio?

POGGIO

Forsooth, my master said that he loved her almost as well
as he loved parmasent, and swore (I'll be sworn for him)
that she wanted but such a nose as his was to be as pretty a
young woman as any was in Parma.   60

DONADO

O gross.

BERGETTO

Nay, uncle, then she asked me whether my father had any

---

42 *thither* ed. hither Q
53 *Uds sa' me* God save me
58 *parmasent* parmesan, the cheese of Parma

---

47 *may-game.* Laughing-stock. Cf. *The Lover's Melancholy*, I.ii, 10
'Why should not I, a May-game, scorn the weight/Of my sunk fortunes?'

more children than myself: and I said 'No, 'twere better
he should have had his brains knocked out first.'

DONADO

This is intolerable.   65

BERGETTO

Then said she 'Will Signor Donado your uncle leave you
all his wealth?'

DONADO

Ha! that was good; did she harp upon that string?

BERGETTO

Did she harp upon that string? Ay, that she did. I answered
'Leave me all his wealth? Why, woman, he hath no other wit;   70
if he had, he should hear on't to his everlasting glory and
confusion: I know,' quoth I, 'I am his white boy, and will
not be gulled'; and with that she fell into a great smile and
went away. Nay, I did fit her.

DONADO

Ah, sirrah, then I see there is no changing of nature. Well,   75
Bergetto, I fear thou wilt be a very ass still.

BERGETTO

I should be sorry for that, uncle.

DONADO

Come, come you home with me. Since you are no better a
speaker, I'll have you write to her after some courtly manner,
and enclose some rich jewel in the letter.   80

BERGETTO

Ay marry, that will be excellent.

DONADO

Peace, innocent.
Once in my time I'll set my wits to school,
If all fail, 'tis but the fortune of a fool.

BERGETTO

Poggio, 'twill do, Poggio.   *Exeunt*   85

Act II, [Scene i]

Enter GIOVANNI *and* ANNABELLA, *as from their chamber*

GIOVANNI

Come Annabella: no more sister now,
But love, a name more gracious; do not blush,

74 *fit her* answer her aptly   82 *innocent* simpleton

---

72 *white boy*. Favourite, pet. For this use of 'white' in the sense of 'highly
prized, precious' see *O.E.D.* White, a 9.

Beauty's sweet wonder, but be proud to know
That yielding thou hast conquered, and inflamed
A heart whose tribute is thy brother's life.   5

ANNABELLA
And mine is his. O, how these stol'n contents
Would print a modest crimson on my cheeks,
Had any but my heart's delight prevailed.

GIOVANNI
I marvel why the chaster of your sex
Should think this pretty toy called maidenhead   10
So strange a loss, when, being lost, 'tis nothing,
And you are still the same.

ANNABELLA   'Tis well for you;
Now you can talk.

GIOVANNI   Music as well consists
In th' ear as in the playing.

ANNABELLA   O, y'are wanton.
Tell on't, y'are best: do.

GIOVANNI   Thou wilt chide me then.   15
Kiss me:—so. Thus hung Jove on Leda's neck,
And sucked divine ambrosia from her lips.
I envy not the mightiest man alive,
But hold myself in being king of thee
More great than were I king of all the world.   20
But I shall lose you, sweetheart.

ANNABELLA   But you shall not.

GIOVANNI
You must be married, mistress.

ANNABELLA   Yes? To whom?

GIOVANNI
Someone must have you.

ANNABELLA   You must.

GIOVANNI   Nay, some other.

---

16 *Thus hung Jove.* Leda was seduced by Jove in the form of a swan. See
   Ovid, *Metamorphoses*, 6, 109. The myth is aptly used by Giovanni as the
   example of an unnatural union the sensationalism of which has been
   dignified by art.

22 *Yes? To whom?* Q reads 'Yes, to whom?' and it is difficult in a modern-
   ised text to suggest the tone of Annabella's reply. Her three speeches
   (21–3) are probably playful repartee, unconscious of Giovanni's
   serious intent. Perhaps the closest tonal analogue to this moment is in
   As You Like It, IV.i, 90ff. The contrast makes her realisation ('Now
   prithee do not speak so') an intensely dramatic point.

ANNABELLA
  Now prithee do not speak so: without jesting,
  You'll make me weep in earnest.
GIOVANNI   What, you will not?   25
  But tell me, sweet, canst thou be dared to swear
  That thou wilt live to me, and to no other?
ANNABELLA
  By both our loves I dare, for didst thou know,
  My Giovanni, how all suitors seem
  To my eyes hateful, thou wouldst trust me then.   30
GIOVANNI
  Enough, I take thy word. Sweet, we must part.
  Remember what thou vowst; keep well my heart.
ANNABELLA
  Will you be gone?
GIOVANNI   I must.
ANNABELLA   When to return?
GIOVANNI
  Soon.
ANNABELLA   Look you do.
GIOVANNI   Farewell.   *Exit*
ANNABELLA
  Go where thou wilt, in mind I'll keep thee here,   35
  And where thou art, I know I shall be there.
  Guardian!

Enter PUTANA

PUTANA
  Child, how is't, child? Well, thank Heaven, ha?
ANNABELLA
  O guardian, what a paradise of joy
  Have I passed over!   40
PUTANA
  Nay, what a paradise of joy have you passed under! Why,
  now I commend thee, charge; fear nothing, sweetheart;
  what though he be your brother? Your brother's a man,
  I hope, and I say still, if a young wench feel the fit upon her,
  let her take anybody, father or brother, all is one.   45
ANNABELLA
  I would not have it known for all the world.
PUTANA
  Nor I, indeed, for the speech of the people; else 'twere
  nothing.
FLORIO *within*
  Daughter Annabella.

ANNABELLA
  O me, my father!—Here, sir!—Reach my work.   50
FLORIO *within*
  What are you doing?
ANNABELLA   So: let him come now.

    Enter FLORIO, RICHARDETTO *like a doctor of physic, and*
         PHILOTIS *with a lute in her hand*

FLORIO
  So hard at work? That's well; you lose no time.
  Look, I have brought you company; here's one,
  A learned doctor lately come from Padua,
  Much skilled in physic, and for that I see   55
  You have of late been sickly, I entreated
  This reverend man to visit you some time.
ANNABELLA
  Y'are very welcome, sir.
RICHARDETTO   I thank you, mistress.
  Loud fame in large report hath spoke your praise
  As well for virtue as perfection: 60
  For which I have been bold to bring with me
  A kinswoman of mine, a maid, for song
  And music one perhaps will give content;
  Please you to know her.
ANNABELLA   They are parts I love,
  And she for them most welcome.
PHILOTIS   Thank you, lady.   65
FLORIO
  Sir, now you know my house, pray make not strange,
  And if you find my daughter need your art,
  I'll be your paymaster.
RICHARDETTO   Sir, what I am
  She shall command.
FLORIO   You shall bind me to you.
  Daughter, I must have conference with you   70
  About some matters that concerns us both.
  Good master doctor, please you but walk in,
  We'll crave a little of your cousin's cunning.
  I think my girl hath not quite forgot
  To touch an instrument: she could have done't.   75
  We'll hear them both.
RICHARDETTO   I'll wait upon you, sir.   *Exeunt*

  54 *Padua* famous for its university's medical school
  55 *for that* because   **64** *parts* abilities   **73** *cunning* skill

[Act II, Scene ii]

Enter SORANZO *in his study reading a book*

SORANZO

   'Love's measure is extreme, the comfort, pain,
   The life unrest, and the reward disdain.'
   What's here? Look't o'er again: 'tis so, so writes
   This smooth licentious poet in his rhymes.
   But Sannazar, thou liest, for had thy bosom   5
   Felt such oppression as is laid on mine,
   Thou wouldst have kissed the rod that made thee smart.
   To work then, happy muse, and contradict
   What Sannazar hath in his envy writ.
   'Love's measure is the mean, sweet his annoys,   10
   His pleasure's life, and his reward all joys.'
   Had Annabella lived when Sannazar
   Did in his brief encomium celebrate
   Venice, that queen of cities, he had left
   That verse which gained him such a sum of gold,   15
   And for one only look from Annabel
   Had writ of her and her diviner cheeks.
   O how my thoughts are—

VASQUES *within*

   Pray forbear; in rules of civility, let me give notice
   on't: I shall be taxed of my neglect of duty and service.   20

SORANZO

   What rude intrusion interrupts my peace?
   Can I be nowhere private?

VASQUES *within*

   Troth you wrong your modesty.

SORANZO

   What's the matter, Vasques? Who is't?

  7 *thee* ed. the Q
 20 *taxed of* blamed for

---

  5 *Sannazar.* Jacopo Sannazaro, an Italian poet, was born in Naples circa
     1456 and died there in 1530. His best known work, the *Arcadia*, was
     well known in England.
 13 *brief encomium.* A short Latin poem in praise of Venice, for which the
     city lavishly rewarded him. It is quoted by Thomas Coryat in *Coryat's
     Crudities* (1611), and Sherman points out (p. 128) that it appears with
     an English translation in a letter from James Howell to Robert Brown
     of the Middle Temple from Venice, 12 August 1621. Ford, as well as
     Brown, was a member of the Middle Temple.

Enter HIPPOLITA *and* VASQUES

HIPPOLITA
'Tis I: 25
Do you know me now? Look, perjured man, on her
Whom thou and thy distracted lust have wronged.
Thy sensual rage of blood hath made my youth
A scorn to men and angels, and shall I
Be now a foil to thy unsated change?   30
Thou knowst, false wanton, when my modest fame
Stood free from stain or scandal, all the charms
Of hell or sorcery could not prevail
Against the honour of my chaster bosom.
Thine eyes did plead in tears, thy tongue in oaths   35
Such and so many, that a heart of steel
Would have been wrought to pity, as was mine:
And shall the conquest of my lawful bed,
My husband's death urged on by his disgrace,
My loss of womanhood, be ill rewarded   40
With hatred and contempt? No; know, Soranzo,
I have a spirit doth as much distaste
The slavery of fearing thee, as thou
Dost loathe the memory of what hath passed.
SORANZO
Nay, dear Hippolita—
HIPPOLITA   Call me not dear,   45
Nor think with supple words to smooth the grossness
Of my abuses; 'tis not your new mistress,
Your goodly Madam Merchant, shall triumph
On my dejection: tell her thus from me,
My birth was nobler and by much more free.   50
SORANZO
You are too violent.
HIPPOLITA   You are too double
In your dissimulation. Seest thou this,

30 *foil . . . change* background for your promiscuity
42 *distaste* dislike
48 *triumph* accented on second syllable

---

48 *Madam Merchant.* Q prints *Madam Merchant* as if to emphasise the
phrase (though Q's use of italic is by no means regular). *O.E.D.* quotes
the line (Madam sb 2d) as an example of 'playful or derisive uses', and
compares *Measure for Measure*, I.ii, 43 'Behold, behold, where Madam
Mitigation comes'. Hippolita is disparaging Annabella's family, and
pointing out that her own birth 'was nobler and by much more free.'

This habit, these black mourning weeds of care?
'Tis thou art cause of this, and hast divorced
My husband from his life and me from him,   55
And made me widow in my widowhood.

SORANZO

Will you yet hear?

HIPPOLITA   More of thy perjuries?
Thy soul is drowned too deeply in those sins;
Thou need'st not add to th' number.

SORANZO   Then I'll leave you;
You are past all rules of sense.

HIPPOLITA   And thou of grace.   60

VASQUES

Fie, mistress, you are not near the limits of reason: if my lord
had a resolution as noble as virtue itself, you take the course
to unedge it all. Sir, I beseech you, do not perplex her;
griefs, alas, will have a vent. I dare undertake Madam
Hippolita will now freely hear you.   65

SORANZO

Talk to a woman frantic! Are these the fruits of your love?

HIPPOLITA

They are the fruits of thy untruth, false man.
Didst thou not swear, whilst yet my husband lived,
That thou wouldst wish no happiness on earth
More than to call me wife? Didst thou not vow,   70
When he should die, to marry me? For which,
The devil in my blood, and thy protests,
Caused me to counsel him to undertake
A voyage to Ligorn, for that we heard
His brother there was dead, and left a daughter   75
Young and unfriended, who, with much ado,
I wished him to bring hither: he did so,
And went; and as thou know'st died on the way.
Unhappy man, to buy his death so dear
With my advice. Yet thou for whom I did it   80
Forget'st thy vows, and leav'st me to my shame.

SORANZO

Who could help this?

HIPPOLITA   Who? Perjured man, thou couldst,

---

57 *thy* Q *a.c.*; the Q *b.c.*
61 *not near* i.e. beyond (but carefully ambiguous)
63 *unedge* blunt
74 *Ligorn* Leghorn (Italian *Livorno*)

If thou hadst faith or love.
SORANZO   You are deceived.
The vows I made, if you remember well,
Were wicked and unlawful: 'twere more sin   85
To keep them than to break them. As for me,
I cannot mask my penitence. Think thou
How much thou hast digressed from honest shame
In bringing of a gentleman to death
Who was thy husband; such a one as he,   90
So noble in his quality, condition,
Learning, behaviour, entertainment, love,
As Parma could not show a braver man.
VASQUES
You do not well; this was not your promise.
SORANZO
I care not; let her know her monstrous life.   95
Ere I'll be servile to so black a sin,
I'll be accursed. Woman, come here no more.
Learn to repent and die, for by my honour
I hate thee and thy lust: you have been too foul.   [Exit]
VASQUES
[Aside] This part has been scurvily played.   100
HIPPOLITA
How foolishly this beast contemns his fate,
And shuns the use of that which I more scorn
Than I once loved, his love. But let him go;
My vengeance shall give comfort to this woe.
                                    She offers to go away
VASQUES
Mistress, mistress, Madam Hippolita, pray, a word or two!   105

100 *scurvily played* badly acted
101 *contemns* despises
104 *this* ed. his Q

84–6 *The vows . . . break them.* St Augustine, in *De bono coniugali* (Corpus
    Scriptorum Ecclesiasticorum Latinorum, Vienna, 1866ff., XLI,
    187ff.), argues that breaking a contract made in sin to return to virtue
    was no sin at all. But this was not everyone's view. See Alan T. Gaylord,
    'The Promises in the Franklin's Tale', *ELH*, XXXI, 4 (1964), 331–65.
97 *accursed.* a Curse Q *b.c.*; a Coarse Q *a.c.* Bawcutt's emendation,
    'accurs'd', has everything to commend it. The three forms could be
    very similar in seventeenth-century handwriting, and 'accursed' gives
    the best sense. It does suggest, however, that Q's press corrections are
    not authorial. Cf. note to IV.iii, 63.

HIPPOLITA
With me, sir?
VASQUES
With you, if you please.
HIPPOLITA
What is't?
VASQUES
I know you are infinitely moved now, and you think you
have cause; some I confess you have, but sure not so much as   110
you imagine.
HIPPOLITA
Indeed.
VASQUES
O, you were miserably bitter, which you followed even to
the last syllable. Faith, you were somewhat too shrewd;
by my life you could not have took my lord in a worse   115
time, since I first knew him: tomorrow you shall find him
a new man.
HIPPOLITA
Well, I shall wait his leisure.
VASQUES
Fie, this is not a hearty patience, it comes sourly from you;
troth, let me persuade you for once.   120
HIPPOLITA
[*Aside*] I have it, and it shall be so; thanks, opportunity!—
Persuade me to what?
VASQUES
Visit him in some milder temper. O if you could but master
a little your female spleen, how might you win him.
HIPPOLITA
He will never love me. Vasques, thou hast been a too   125
trusty servant to such a master, and I believe thy reward
in the end will fall out like mine.
VASQUES
So perhaps too.
HIPPOLITA
Resolve thyself it will. Had I one so true, so truly honest,
so secret to my counsels, as thou hast been to him and his,   130
I should think it a slight acquittance, not only to make him
master of all I have, but even of myself.

114 *shrewd* scolding
129 *Resolve* Assure
131 *acquittance* discharge of debt

VASQUES

O you are a noble gentlewoman.

HIPPOLITA

Wilt thou feed always upon hopes? Well, I know thou art
wise, and seest the reward of an old servant daily, what it is.   135

VASQUES

Beggary and neglect.

HIPPOLITA

True: but Vasques, wert thou mine, and wouldst be
private to me and my designs, I here protest myself and all
what I can else call mine should be at thy dispose.

VASQUES

[*Aside*] Work you that way, old mole? Then I have the wind   140
of you.—I were not worthy of it by any desert that could lie
within my compass; if I could—

HIPPOLITA

What then?

VASQUES

I should then hope to live in these my old years with rest
and security.   145

HIPPOLITA

Give me thy hand: now promise but thy silence,
And help to bring to pass a plot I have,
And here in sight of Heaven, that being done,
I make thee lord of me and mine estate.

VASQUES

Come, you are merry; this is such a happiness that I can   150
neither think or believe.

HIPPOLITA

Promise thy secrecy, and 'tis confirmed.

VASQUES

Then here I call our good genii for witnesses, whatsoever
your designs are, or against whomsoever, I will not only be
a special actor therein, but never disclose it till it be effected.   155

HIPPOLITA

I take thy word, and with that, thee for mine;
Come then, let's more confer of this anon.
On this delicious bane my thoughts shall banquet:
Revenge shall sweeten what my griefs have tasted.   *Exeunt*

140 *have the wind* understand your intention
153 *for witnesses* ed. foe-witnesses Q
158 *bane* poison

[Act II, Scene iii]

Enter RICHARDETTO *and* PHILOTIS

RICHARDETTO
Thou seest, my lovely niece, these strange mishaps,
How all my fortunes turn to my disgrace,
Wherein I am but as a looker-on,
Whiles others act my shame, and I am silent.

PHILOTIS
But uncle, wherein can this borrowed shape   5
Give you content?

RICHARDETTO   I'll tell thee, gentle niece:
Thy wanton aunt in her lascivious riots
Lives now secure, thinks I am surely dead
In my late journey to Ligorn for you
(As I have caused it to be rumoured out).   10
Now would I see with what an impudence
She gives scope to her loose adultery,
And how the common voice allows hereof:
Thus far I have prevailed.

PHILOTIS   Alas, I fear
You mean some strange revenge.

RICHARDETTO   O, be not troubled;   15
Your ignorance shall plead for you in all.
But to our business: what, you learned for certain
How Signor Florio means to give his daughter
In marriage to Soranzo?

PHILOTIS   Yes, for certain.

RICHARDETTO
But how find you young Annabella's love   20
Inclined to him?

PHILOTIS   For aught I could perceive,
She neither fancies him or any else.

RICHARDETTO
There's mystery in that which time must show.
She used you kindly?

PHILOTIS   Yes.

RICHARDETTO   And craved your company?

PHILOTIS
Often.

5 *borrowed shape* disguise
13 *how . . . hereof* what people say about it
16 *Your . . . all* The less you know the better

RICHARDETTO   'Tis well; it goes as I could wish.   25
    I am the doctor now, and as for you,
    None knows you; if all fail not, we shall thrive.
    But who comes here?

                    Enter GRIMALDI

                    I know him: 'tis Grimaldi,
    A Roman and a soldier, near allied
    Unto the duke of Montferrato, one   30
    Attending on the nuncio of the Pope
    That now resides in Parma, by which means
    He hopes to get the love of Annabella.
GRIMALDI
    Save you, sir.
RICHARDETTO   And you, sir.
GRIMALDI   I have heard
    Of your approved skill, which through the city   35
    Is freely talked of, and would crave your aid.
RICHARDETTO
    For what, sir?
GRIMALDI   Marry, sir, for this—
    But I would speak in private.
RICHARDETTO   Leave us, cousin.
                                    Exit PHILOTIS

GRIMALDI
    I love fair Annabella, and would know
    Whether in art there may not be receipts   40
    To move affection.
RICHARDETTO   Sir, perhaps there may,
    But these will nothing profit you.
GRIMALDI   Not me?
RICHARDETTO
    Unless I be mistook, you are a man
    Greatly in favour with the cardinal.
GRIMALDI
    What of that?
RICHARDETTO   In duty to his grace,   45
    I will be bold to tell you, if you seek
    To marry Florio's daughter, you must first
    Remove a bar 'twixt you and her.
GRIMALDI   Who's that?

    35 *through* pronounced 'thorough'
    40 *art* ed. Arts Q
    40 *receipts* recipes (love-potions)

RICHARDETTO
Soranzo is the man that hath her heart;
And while he lives, be sure you cannot speed.   50
GRIMALDI
Soranzo! What, mine enemy! Is't he?
RICHARDETTO
Is he your enemy?
GRIMALDI   The man I hate
Worse than confusion;
I'll kill him straight.
RICHARDETTO   Nay then, take mine advice
(Even for his grace's sake, the cardinal):   55
I'll find a time when he and she do meet,
Of which I'll give you notice, and to be sure
He shall not 'scape you, I'll provide a poison
To dip your rapier's point in; if he had
As many heads as Hydra had, he dies.   60
GRIMALDI
But shall I trust thee, doctor?
RICHARDETTO   As yourself;
Doubt not in aught. [*Aside*] Thus shall the fates decree:
By me Soranzo falls, that ruined me.   *Exeunt*

[Act II, Scene iv]

Enter DONADO, BERGETTO *and* POGGIO

DONADO
Well, sir, I must be content to be both your secretary and
your messenger myself. I cannot tell what this letter may
work, but as sure as I am alive, if thou come once to talk
with her, I fear thou wilt mar whatsoever I make.
BERGETTO
You make, uncle? Why, am not I big enough to carry mine   5
own letter, I pray?
DONADO
Ay, ay, carry a fool's head o' thy own. Why, thou dunce,
wouldst thou write a letter and carry it thyself?
BERGETTO
Yes, that I would, and read it to her with my own mouth;
for you must think, if she will not believe me myself when   10
she hears me speak, she will not believe another's hand-

50 *speed* succeed
54 *kill* Q *a.c.*; tell Q *b.c.*
63 *ruined* ruin'd Q *a.c.*; min'd Q *b.c.*

writing. O, you think I am a blockhead, uncle. No, sir,
Poggio knows I have indited a letter myself, so I have.

POGGIO

Yes truly, sir; I have it in my pocket.

DONADO

A sweet one, no doubt; pray let's see't.   15

BERGETTO

I cannot read my own hand very well, Poggio; read it,
Poggio.

DONADO

Begin.

POGGIO *reads*

'Most dainty and honey-sweet mistress, I could call
you fair, and lie as fast as any that loves you, but my uncle   20
being the elder man, I leave it to him, as more fit for his age
and the colour of his beard. I am wise enough to tell you I
can bourd where I see occasion; or if you like my uncle's
wit better than mine, you shall marry me; if you like mine
better than his, I will marry you in spite of your teeth. So   25
commending my best parts to you, I rest—Yours upwards
and downwards, or you may choose, Bergetto.'

BERGETTO

Aha, here's stuff, uncle.

DONADO

Here's stuff indeed to shame us all. Pray whose advice did
you take in this learned letter?   30

POGGIO

None, upon my word, but mine own.

BERGETTO

And mine, uncle, believe it, nobody's else; 'twas mine own
brain, I thank a good wit for't.

DONADO

Get you home, sir, and look you keep within doors till I
return.   35

BERGETTO

How! That were a jest indeed; I scorn it i'faith.

DONADO

What! You do not?

BERGETTO

Judge me, but I do now.

POGGIO

Indeed, sir, 'tis very unhealthy.

23 *bourd* jest

DONADO

    Well, sir, if I hear any of your apish running to motions   40
    and fopperies, till I come back, you were as good no; look
    to't.   *Exit* DONADO

BERGETTO

    Poggio, shall's steal to see this horse with the head in's tail?

POGGIO

    Ay, but you must take heed of whipping.

BERGETTO

    Dost take me for a child, Poggio? Come, honest Poggio.   45
                                     Exeunt

[Act II, Scene v]

Enter FRIAR *and* GIOVANNI

FRIAR

    Peace. Thou hast told a tale, whose every word
    Threatens eternal slaughter to the soul.
    I'm sorry I have heard it; would mine ears
    Had been one minute deaf, before the hour
    That thou cam'st to me. O young man castaway,   5
    By the religious number of mine order,
    I day and night have waked my aged eyes,
    Above my strength, to weep on thy behalf:
    But Heaven is angry, and be thou resolved,
    Thou art a man remarked to taste a mischief.   10
    Look for't; though it come late, it will come sure.

GIOVANNI

    Father, in this you are uncharitable;
    What I have done I'll prove both fit and good.

   40 *motions* puppet shows
    8 *my* ed. thy Q
    9 *resolved* assured
   10 *remarked* marked out
   10 *mischief* disaster

    6 *By the religious* etc. The text may well be corrupt here. 'Number' has
    been explained as 'group' or 'company', but the subdued oath would be
    an odd one, and even odder in Gifford's emendation of 'number' to
    'founder'. I would tentatively suggest moving the comma after 'cast-
    away' (line 5) and placing it after 'man', thus emphasising the point
    that the Friar makes (I.i, 53–5) that he has left all to follow Giovanni.

It is a principle (which you have taught
When I was yet your scholar), that the frame   15
And composition of the mind doth follow
The frame and composition of the body:
So where the body's furniture is beauty,
The mind's must needs be virtue; which allowed,
Virtue itself is reason but refined,   20
And love the quintessence of that. This proves
My sister's beauty being rarely fair
Is rarely virtuous; chiefly in her love,
And chiefly in that love, her love to me.
If hers to me, then so is mine to her;   25
Since in like causes are effects alike.

FRIAR

O ignorance in knowledge. Long ago,
How often have I warned thee this before?
Indeed, if we were sure there were no deity,
Nor Heaven nor hell, then to be led alone   30
By nature's light (as were philosophers
Of elder times), might instance some defence.
But 'tis not so; then, madman, thou wilt find
That nature is in Heaven's positions blind.

GIOVANNI

Your age o'errules you; had you youth like mine,   35
You'd make her love your Heaven, and her divine.

FRIAR

Nay then, I see th'art too far sold to hell,
It lies not in the compass of my prayers

15 *frame* ed. Fame Q
17 *the body* ed. Body Q
34 *positions* propositions, doctrines

14–19 *It is a principle* etc. Cf. Spenser, *An Hymne in Honour of Beautie*,
132–3:

> For of the soule the bodie forme doth take:
> For soule is forme, and doth the bodie make.

Giovanni's argument brings together a number of vaguely neoplatonic
ideas about the relationship of the good to the beautiful, but forms no
proper links between them. Cf. Ford's *Honour Triumphant*, Third
Position (*Works*, ed. Gifford—Dyce, iii, 359), and Tilley F1.

31–2 *philosophers Of elder times*. Pre-Christian philosophers. Cf. Donne,
Satire III, 11–15. It was sometimes argued by theologians that pagan
philosophers, who followed the light of nature, would thus come to
salvation by 'imputed' grace.

34 *That nature* etc. i.e. to study nature teaches us nothing about God.

To call thee back; yet let me counsel thee:
Persuade thy sister to some marriage.   40
GIOVANNI
Marriage? Why, that's to damn her. That's to prove
Her greedy of variety of lust.
FRIAR
O fearful! If thou wilt not, give me leave
To shrive her, lest she should die unabsolved.
GIOVANNI
At your best leisure, father; then she'll tell you   45
How dearly she doth prize my matchless love.
Then you will know what pity 'twere we two
Should have been sundered from each other's arms.
View well her face, and in that little round
You may observe a world of variety: 50
For colour, lips; for sweet perfumes, her breath;
For jewels, eyes; for threads of purest gold,
Hair; for delicious choice of flowers, cheeks;
Wonder in every portion of that throne.
Hear her but speak, and you will swear the spheres   55
Make music to the citizens in Heaven.
But, father, what is else for pleasure framed,
Lest I offend your ears, shall go unnamed.
FRIAR
The more I hear, I pity thee the more,
That one so excellent should give those parts   60
All to a second death; what I can do
Is but to pray: and yet I could advise thee,
Wouldst thou be ruled.
GIOVANNI   In what?
FRIAR   Why, leave her yet;
The throne of mercy is above your trespass;
Yet time is left you both—
GIOVANNI   To embrace each other,   65
Else let all time be struck quite out of number.
She is like me, and I like her, resolved.
FRIAR
No more! I'll visit her. This grieves me most,
Things being thus, a pair of souls are lost.   *Exeunt*

61 *second death* damnation

[Act II, Scene vi]

Enter FLORIO, DONADO, ANNABELLA, PUTANA

FLORIO
Where's Giovanni?

ANNABELLA   Newly walked abroad,
And, as I heard him say, gone to the friar,
His reverend tutor.

FLORIO   That's a blessed man,
A man made up of holiness; I hope
He'll teach him how to gain another world.   5

DONADO
Fair gentlewoman, here's a letter sent
To you from my young cousin; I dare swear
He loves you in his soul: would you could hear
Sometimes what I see daily, sighs and tears,
As if his breast were prison to his heart.   10

FLORIO
Receive it, Annabella.

ANNABELLA
Alas, good man.

DONADO
What's that she said?

PUTANA
An't please you, sir, she said, 'Alas, good man.' Truly I
do commend him to her every night before her first sleep,   15
because I would have her dream of him, and she hearkens
to that most religiously.

DONADO
Say'st so? God-a-mercy, Putana, there's something for thee,
and prithee do what thou canst on his behalf; sha' not be
lost labour, take my word for't.   20

PUTANA
Thank you most heartily, sir; now I have a feeling of your
mind, let me alone to work.

ANNABELLA
Guardian!

PUTANA
Did you call?

ANNABELLA
Keep this letter.   25

14 *An't* ed. And Q

DONADO
Signor Florio, in any case bid her read it instantly.

FLORIO
Keep it for what? Pray read it me hereright.

ANNABELLA
I shall, sir.   *She reads*

DONADO
How d'ee find her inclined, signor?

FLORIO
Troth, sir, I know not how; not all so well   30
As I could wish.

ANNABELLA
Sir, I am bound to rest your cousin's debtor.
The jewel I'll return; for if he love,
I'll count that love a jewel.

DONADO   Mark you that?
Nay, keep them both, sweet maid.

ANNABELLA   You must excuse me,   35
Indeed I will not keep it.

FLORIO   Where's the ring,
That which your mother in her will bequeathed,
And charged you on her blessing not to give't
To any but your husband? Send back that.

ANNABELLA
I have it not.

FLORIO   Ha, have it not! Where is't?   40

ANNABELLA
My brother in the morning took it from me,
Said he would wear't today.

FLORIO   Well, what do you say
To young Bergetto's love? Are you content
To match with him? Speak.

DONADO   There's the point indeed.

ANNABELLA
[*Aside*] What shall I do? I must say something now.   45

---

27 *hereright* straightaway

---

39 *Send back that.* Florio's conduct has been sharply judged: 'Florio
juggles strangely with his daughter's suitors. He tells Soranzo in Act I
that he had "his word engaged;" and yet here he endeavours to force
her upon another! His subsequent conduct is not calculated to increase
our respect for his character, or our sympathy for his overwhelming
afflictions.' (Gifford). But perhaps Florio's hypocrisy is no more than
tact.

FLORIO
    What say? Why d'ee not speak?
ANNABELLA   Sir, with your leave,
    Please you to give me freedom?
FLORIO   Yes, you have it.
ANNABELLA
    Signor Donado, if your nephew mean
    To raise his better fortunes in his match,
    The hope of me will hinder such a hope;   50
    Sir, if you love him, as I know you do,
    Find one more worthy of his choice than me.
    In short, I'm sure I sha' not be his wife.
DONADO
    Why, here's plain dealing; I commend thee for't,
    And all the worst I wish thee is, Heaven bless thee!   55
    Your father yet and I will still be friends,
    Shall we not, Signor Florio?
FLORIO   Yes, why not?
    Look, here your cousin comes.

Enter BERGETTO *and* POGGIO

DONADO
    [*Aside*] O coxcomb, what doth he make here?
BERGETTO
    Where's my uncle, sirs?   60
DONADO
    What's the news now?
BERGETTO
    Save you, uncle, save you. You must not think I come for
    nothing, masters; and how, and how is't? What, you have
    read my letter? Ah, there I—tickled you i'faith.
POGGIO
    But 'twere better you had tickled her in another place.   65
BERGETTO
    Sirrah sweetheart, I'll tell thee a good jest; and riddle what
    'tis.
ANNABELLA
    You say you'd tell me.
BERGETTO
    As I was walking just now in the street, I met a swaggering
    fellow would needs take the wall of me, and because he   70

47 *have it* ed. have Q
70 *take the wall* jostle off the pavement

did thrust me, I very valiantly called him rogue. He here-
upon bade me draw; I told him I had more wit than so,
but when he saw that I would not, he did so maul me with
the hilts of his rapier that my head sung whilst my feet
capered in the kennel.   75

DONADO

[*Aside*] Was ever the like ass seen?

ANNABELLA

And what did you all this while?

BERGETTO

Laugh at him for a gull, till I see the blood run about
mine ears, and then I could not choose but find in my
heart to cry; till a fellow with a broad beard (they say he   80
is a new-come doctor) called me into his house, and gave
me a plaster—look you, here 'tis—and, sir, there was a
young wench washed my face and hands most excellently,
i'faith, I shall love her as long as I live for't, did she not,
Poggio?   85

POGGIO

Yes, and kissed him too.

BERGETTO

Why, la now, you think I tell a lie, uncle, I warrant.

DONADO

Would he that beat thy blood out of thy head had beaten
some wit into it; for I fear thou never wilt have any.

BERGETTO

O, uncle, but there was a wench would have done a man's   90
heart good to have looked on her—by this light she had a
face methinks worth twenty of you, Mistress Annabella.

DONADO

Was ever such a fool born?

ANNABELLA

I am glad she liked you, sir.

BERGETTO

Are you so? By my troth I thank you, forsooth.   95

FLORIO

Sure 'twas the doctor's niece, that was last day with us here.

BERGETTO

'Twas she, 'twas she.

75 *kennel* gutter
78 *gull* dupe, simpleton
81 *his* ed. this Q
94 *liked* pleased

DONADO
How do you know that, simplicity?

BERGETTO
Why, does not he say so? If I should have said no, I should
have given him the lie, uncle, and so have deserved a dry   100
beating again; I'll none of that.

FLORIO
A very modest well-behaved young maid
As I have seen.

DONADO   Is she indeed?

FLORIO   Indeed
She is, if I have any judgment.

DONADO
Well, sir, now you are free, you need not care for sending   105
letters: now you are dismissed, your mistress here will none
of you.

BERGETTO
No. Why, what care I for that? I can have wenches enough
in Parma for half-a-crown apiece, cannot I, Poggio?

POGGIO
I'll warrant you, sir.   110

DONADO
Signor Florio,
I thank you for your free recourse you gave
For my admittance; and to you, fair maid,
That jewel I will give you 'gainst your marriage.
Come, will you go, sir?   115

BERGETTO
Ay, marry will I. Mistress, farewell, mistress. I'll come
again tomorrow. Farewell, mistress.

Exit DONADO, BERGETTO, *and* POGGIO

Enter GIOVANNI

FLORIO
Son, where have you been? What, alone, alone still?
I would not have it so, you must forsake
This over-bookish humour. Well, your sister   120
Hath shook the fool off.

GIOVANNI   'Twas no match for her.

FLORIO
'Twas not indeed, I meant it nothing less;

100 *dry* severe, bruising (not drawing blood)
114 *'gainst* in anticipation of
118 *still* ed. still, still Q

Soranzo is the man I only like—
Look on him, Annabella. Come, 'tis supper-time,
And it grows late.   *Exit* FLORIO   125
GIOVANNI
Whose jewel's that?
ANNABELLA   Some sweetheart's.
GIOVANNI   So I think.
ANNABELLA
A lusty youth,
Signor Donado, gave it me to wear
Against my marriage.
GIOVANNI   But you shall not wear it.
Send it him back again.
ANNABELLA   What, you are jealous?   130
GIOVANNI
That you shall know anon, at better leisure.
Welcome, sweet night! The evening crowns the day.
                                               Exeunt

Act III, [Scene i]

Enter BERGETTO *and* POGGIO

BERGETTO
Does my uncle think to make me a baby still? No, Poggio,
he shall know I have a sconce now.
POGGIO
Ay, let him not bob you off like an ape with an apple.
BERGETTO
'Sfoot, I will have the wench if he were ten uncles, in despite
of his nose, Poggio.   5
POGGIO
Hold him to the grindstone and give not a jot of ground.
She hath in a manner promised you already.
BERGETTO
True, Poggio, and her uncle the doctor swore I should
marry her.
POGGIO
He swore, I remember.   10

123 *only* specially, singularly
  2 *sconce* brain
  3 *bob* fob
  8 s.p. BERGETTO ed. Poggio Q

---

132 *The evening crowns the day.* Proverbial. Tilley E190.

BERGETTO

And I will have her, that's more; didst see the codpiece-
point she gave me and the box of marmalade?

POGGIO

Very well; and kissed you, that my chops watered at the
sight on't. There's no way but to clap up a marriage in
hugger-mugger. 15

BERGETTO

I will do't; for I tell thee, Poggio, I begin to grow valiant
methinks, and my courage begins to rise.

POGGIO

Should you be afraid of your uncle?

BERGETTO

Hang him, old doting rascal. No, I say I will have her.

POGGIO

Lose no time then. 20

BERGETTO

I will beget a race of wise men and constables, that shall
cart whores at their own charges, and break the duke's
peace ere I have done myself.—Come away.   *Exeunt*

[Act III, Scene ii]

Enter FLORIO, GIOVANNI, SORANZO, ANNABELLA, PUTANA
and VASQUES

FLORIO

My Lord Soranzo, though I must confess
The proffers that are made me have been great
In marriage of my daughter, yet the hope
Of your still rising honours have prevailed
Above all other jointures. Here she is; 5
She knows my mind, speak for yourself to her,
And hear you, daughter, see you use him nobly;
For any private speech I'll give you time.
Come, son, and you the rest, let them alone:
Agree they as they may.

SORANZO   I thank you, sir. 10

GIOVANNI

[*Aside*] Sister, be not all woman, think on me.

11–12 *codpiece-point* ornamental lace for tying codpiece
14 *clap up* make or settle hastily
15 *in hugger-mugger* secretly, clandestinely
22 *cart whores* exhibit them in streets, as part of punishment
10 *Agree they* ed. Agree Q

SORANZO
  Vasques.
VASQUES
  My lord?
SORANZO
  Attend me without.

Exeunt omnes, manet SORANZO *and* ANNABELLA

ANNABELLA
  Sir, what's your will with me?
SORANZO   Do you not know   15
  What I should tell you?
ANNABELLA   Yes, you'll say you love me.
SORANZO
  And I'll swear it too; will you believe it?
ANNABELLA
  'Tis no point of faith.

Enter GIOVANNI *above*

SORANZO   Have you not will to love?
ANNABELLA
  Not you.
SORANZO   Whom then?
ANNABELLA   That's as the fates infer.
GIOVANNI
  [*Aside*] Of those I'm regent now.
SORANZO   What mean you, sweet?   20
ANNABELLA
  To live and die a maid.
SORANZO   O, that's unfit.
GIOVANNI
  [*Aside*] Here's one can say that's but a woman's note.
SORANZO
  Did you but see my heart, then would you swear—
ANNABELLA
  That you were dead.
GIOVANNI [*Aside*]   That's true, or somewhat near it.
SORANZO
  See you these true love's tears?
ANNABELLA   No.
GIOVANNI [*Aside*]   Now she winks.   25
SORANZO
  They plead to you for grace.
ANNABELLA   Yet nothing speak.

18 *no* ed. not Q   18 *point of faith* dogma necessary to salvation

SORANZO
  O grant my suit.
ANNABELLA   What is't?
SORANZO   To let me live—
ANNABELLA
  Take it.
SORANZO   —Still yours.
ANNABELLA   That is not mine to give.
GIOVANNI
  [*Aside*] One such another word would kill his hopes.
SORANZO
  Mistress, to leave those fruitless strifes of wit,   30
  Know I have loved you long and loved you truly;
  Not hope of what you have, but what you are,
  Have drawn me on; then let me not in vain
  Still feel the rigour of your chaste disdain.
  I'm sick, and sick to th' heart.
ANNABELLA   Help, aqua-vitae.   35
SORANZO
  What mean you?
ANNABELLA   Why, I thought you had been sick.
SORANZO
  Do you mock my love?
GIOVANNI [*Aside*]   There, sir, she was too nimble.
SORANZO
  [*Aside*] 'Tis plain, she laughs at me.—These scornful taunts
  Neither become your modesty or years.
ANNABELLA
  You are no looking glass; or if you were,   40
  I'd dress my language by you.
GIOVANNI [*Aside*]   I'm confirmed.
ANNABELLA
  To put you out of doubt, my lord, methinks
  Your common sense should make you understand
  That if I loved you, or desired your love,
  Some way I should have given you better taste: 45
  But since you are a nobleman, and one
  I would not wish should spend his youth in hopes,
  Let me advise you here to forbear your suit,
  And think I wish you well, I tell you this.
SORANZO
  Is't you speak this?

31 *Know* ed. I know Q
35 *aqua-vitae* spirits, used here as a restorative

ANNABELLA   Yes, I myself; yet know—   50
  Thus far I give you comfort—if mine eyes
  Could have picked out a man (amongst all those
  That sued to me) to make a husband of,
  You should have been that man. Let this suffice;
  Be noble in your secrecy and wise.   55

GIOVANNI
  [*Aside*] Why, now I see she loves me.

ANNABELLA   One word more:
  As ever virtue lived within your mind,
  As ever noble courses were your guide,
  As ever you would have me know you loved me,
  Let not my father know hereof by you;   60
  If I hereafter find that I must marry,
  It shall be you or none.

SORANZO   I take that promise.

ANNABELLA
  O, O, my head.

SORANZO
  What's the matter? Not well?

ANNABELLA
  O, I begin to sicken.   65

GIOVANNI
  [*Aside*] Heaven forbid.   *Exit from above*

SORANZO
  Help, help within there, ho!

        Enter FLORIO, GIOVANNI, PUTANA

  Look to your daughter, Signor Florio.

FLORIO
  Hold her up, she swoons.

GIOVANNI
  Sister, how d'ee?   70

ANNABELLA
  Sick—brother, are you there?

FLORIO
  Convey her to her bed instantly, whilst I send for a physician;
  quickly, I say.

PUTANA
  Alas, poor child!   *Exeunt, manet* SORANZO

           Enter VASQUES

67 s.d. ed.; after line 68 in Q
68 assigned to Soranzo since Gifford's ed.; to Giovanni in Q

VASQUES

  My lord.   75

SORANZO

  O Vasques, now I doubly am undone
  Both in my present and my future hopes.
  She plainly told me that she could not love,
  And thereupon soon sickened, and I fear
  Her life's in danger.   80

VASQUES

  [*Aside*] By'r lady, sir, and so is yours, if you knew all.—
  'Las, sir, I am sorry for that; may be 'tis but the maid's-
  sickness, an over-flux of youth, and then, sir, there is no such
  present remedy as present marriage. But hath she given you
  an absolute denial?   85

SORANZO

  She hath and she hath not; I'm full of grief,
  But what she said I'll tell thee as we go.   *Exeunt*

[Act III, Scene iii]

Enter GIOVANNI *and* PUTANA

PUTANA

  O sir, we are all undone, quite undone, utterly undone, and
  shamed forever; your sister, O your sister.

GIOVANNI

  What of her? For Heaven's sake, speak; how does she?

PUTANA

  O that ever I was born to see this day.

GIOVANNI

  She is not dead, ha? Is she?   5

PUTANA

  Dead? No, she is quick; 'tis worse, she is with child. You
  know what you have done; Heaven forgive 'ee. 'Tis too late
  to repent now, Heaven help us.

GIOVANNI

  With child? How dost thou know't?

PUTANA

  How do I know't? Am I at these years ignorant what the   10
  meanings of qualms and water-pangs be? Of changing of
  colours, queasiness of stomachs, pukings, and another
  thing that I could name? Do not, for her and your credit's

82–3 *maid's-sickness* green-sickness, chlorosis, a form of anaemia
83 *over-flux* overflow
6 *quick* both 'alive' and 'pregnant'

sake, spend the time in asking how, and which way, 'tis so;
she is quick, upon my word: if you let a physician see her   15
water, y'are undone.

GIOVANNI

But in what case is she?

PUTANA

Prettily amended; 'twas but a fit which I soon espied, and
she must look for often henceforward.

GIOVANNI

Commend me to her, bid her take no care;   20
Let not the doctor visit her, I charge you,
Make some excuse, till I return.—O me!
I have a world of business in my head.—
Do not discomfort her.—
How does this news perplex me!—If my father   25
Come to her, tell him she's recovered well,
Say 'twas but some ill diet; d'ee hear, woman?
Look you to't.

PUTANA

I will, sir.   *Exeunt*

[Act III, Scene iv]

Enter FLORIO *and* RICHARDETTO

FLORIO

And how d'ee find her, sir?

RICHARDETTO   Indifferent well;
I see no danger, scarce perceive she's sick,
But that she told me she had lately eaten
Melons, and, as she thought, those disagreed
With her young stomach.

FLORIO   Did you give her aught?   5

RICHARDETTO

An easy surfeit-water, nothing else.
You need not doubt her health; I rather think
Her sickness is a fulness of her blood—
You understand me?

FLORIO   I do; you counsel well,

17 *case* state
20 *take no care* not worry
25 *does* ed. doe Q
 1 *Indifferent* Fairly
 6 *surfeit-water* cure for indigestion

And once, within these few days, will so order't   10
She shall be married ere she know the time.

RICHARDETTO
Yet let not haste, sir, make unworthy choice;
That were dishonour.

FLORIO   Master Doctor, no;
I will not do so neither; in plain words,
My Lord Soranzo is the man I mean.   15

RICHARDETTO
A noble and a virtuous gentleman.

FLORIO
As any is in Parma. Not far hence
Dwells Father Bonaventure, a grave friar,
Once tutor to my son; now at his cell
I'll have 'em married.

RICHARDETTO   You have plotted wisely.   20

FLORIO
I'll send one straight to speak with him tonight.

RICHARDETTO
Soranzo's wise, he will delay no time.

FLORIO
It shall be so.

Enter FRIAR *and* GIOVANNI

FRIAR   Good peace be here and love.

FLORIO
Welcome, religious friar; you are one
That still bring blessing to the place you come to.   25

GIOVANNI
Sir, with what speed I could, I did my best
To draw this holy man from forth his cell
To visit my sick sister, that with words
Of ghostly comfort, in this time of need,
He might absolve her, whether she live or die.   30

FLORIO
'Twas well done, Giovanni; thou herein
Hast showed a Christian's care, a brother's love.
Come, father, I'll conduct you to her chamber,
And one thing would entreat you.

FRIAR   Say on, sir.

25 *still* always
29 *ghostly* spiritual

FLORIO

    I have a father's dear impression,   35
    And wish, before I fall into my grave,
    That I might see her married, as 'tis fit;
    A word from you, grave man, will win her more
    Than all our best persuasions.

FRIAR   Gentle sir,
    All this I'll say, that Heaven may prosper her.   *Exeunt*   40

[Act III, Scene v]

Enter GRIMALDI

GRIMALDI

    Now if the doctor keep his word, Soranzo,
    Twenty to one you miss your bride; I know
    'Tis an unnoble act, and not becomes
    A soldier's valour, but in terms of love,
    Where merit cannot sway, policy must.   5
    I am resolved; if this physician
    Play not on both hands, then Soranzo falls.

Enter RICHARDETTO

RICHARDETTO

    You are come as I could wish; this very night
    Soranzo, 'tis ordained, must be affied
    To Annabella, and, for aught I know,   10
    Married.

GRIMALDI   How!

RICHARDETTO   Yet your patience:—
    The place, 'tis Friar Bonaventure's cell.
    Now I would wish you to bestow this night
    In watching thereabouts; 'tis but a night:
    If you miss now, tomorrow I'll know all.   15

---

5 *policy* cunning
7 *Play . . . hands* Does not double cross me
9 *affied* betrothed
12 *Friar* ed. Fryars Q

---

35 *impression.* Notion, idea, belief impressed on the mind—*O.E.D.* 7,
    quoting 1613 PURCHAS *Pilgrimage* (1614) 2 'That there is a God;
    . . . This is a common notion, and impression, sealed up in the minde
    of every man.' Bawcutt says 'The meaning is not clear.'
14–15 *'tis but . . . all.* i.e. you only risk wasting a night: if nothing happens
    I shall learn the full details tomorrow, and instruct you accordingly.

GRIMALDI
  Have you the poison?
RICHARDETTO   Here 'tis in this box.
  Doubt nothing, this will do't; in any case,
  As you respect your life, be quick and sure.
GRIMALDI
  I'll speed him.
RICHARDETTO   Do. Away; for 'tis not safe
  You should be seen much here.—Ever my love!   20
GRIMALDI
  And mine to you.   *Exit* GRIMALDI
RICHARDETTO
  So. If this hit, I'll laugh and hug revenge;
  And they that now dream of a wedding-feast
  May chance to mourn the lusty bridegroom's ruin.
  But to my other business.—Niece Philotis!   25

Enter PHILOTIS

PHILOTIS
  Uncle?
RICHARDETTO
  My lovely niece,
  You have bethought 'ee?
PHILOTIS   Yes, and, as you counselled,
  Fashioned my heart to love him; but he swears
  He will tonight be married, for he fears   30
  His uncle else, if he should know the drift,
  Will hinder all, and call his coz to shrift.
RICHARDETTO
  Tonight? Why, best of all;—but let me see,
  I—ha—yes—so it shall be; in disguise
  We'll early to the friar's, I have thought on't.   35

Enter BERGETTO *and* POGGIO

PHILOTIS
  Uncle, he comes.
RICHARDETTO   Welcome, my worthy coz.
BERGETTO
  Lass, pretty lass, come buss, lass!—Aha, Poggio!
                                        [*Kisses her*]

22 *hit* succeed
37 *buss* kiss

POGGIO

   There's hope of this yet.

RICHARDETTO

   You shall have time enough; withdraw a little,
   We must confer at large.   40

BERGETTO

   Have you not sweetmeats or dainty devices for me?

PHILOTIS

   You shall have enough, sweetheart.

BERGETTO

   Sweetheart! Mark that, Poggio. By my troth, I cannot
   choose but kiss thee once more for that word 'sweetheart.'—
   Poggio, I have a monstrous swelling about my stomach,   45
   whatsoever the matter be.

POGGIO

   You shall have physic for't, sir.

RICHARDETTO

   Time runs apace.

BERGETTO

   Time's a blockhead.

RICHARDETTO

   Be ruled; when we have done what's fit to do,   50
   Then you may kiss your fill, and bed her too.   *Exeunt*

[Act III, Scene vi]

Enter the FRIAR *sitting in a chair,* ANNABELLA *kneeling and*
whispering to him; a table before them and wax-lights; she
weeps and wrings her hands

FRIAR

   I am glad to see this penance; for, believe me,
   You have unripped a soul so foul and guilty
   As I must tell you true, I marvel how
   The earth hath borne you up; but weep, weep on,

40 *at large* at length, fully
42 *shall have* ed. shall Q
s.d. FRIAR ed. Fryar in his study Q (see III.iv, 33)
 2 *unripped* exposed

---

38 s.p. POGGIO. Assigned to Poggio by Bawcutt; Q (obviously wrongly)
   assigns it to Philotis, and earlier editors to Richardetto.
s.d. Ford frequently sets a scene with considerable exactness, and an eye for
   significant stage-detail. Cf. *Love's Sacrifice*, III.iv, and V.iii, or *The*
   Broken Heart, V.iii.

These tears may do you good; weep faster yet,   5
Whiles I do read a lecture.

ANNABELLA   Wretched creature!

FRIAR
Ay, you are wretched, miserably wretched,
Almost condemned alive. There is a place—
List, daughter—in a black and hollow vault,
Where day is never seen; there shines no sun,   10
But flaming horror of consuming fires,
A lightless sulphur, choked with smoky fogs
Of an infected darkness; in this place
Dwell many thousand thousand sundry sorts
Of never-dying deaths; there damned souls   15
Roar without pity; there are gluttons fed
With toads and adders; there is burning oil
Poured down the drunkard's throat; the usurer
Is forced to sup whole draughts of molten gold;
There is the murderer forever stabbed,   20
Yet can he never die; there lies the wanton
On racks of burning steel, whiles in his soul
He feels the torment of his raging lust.

ANNABELLA
Mercy, O mercy!

FRIAR   There stands these wretched things
Who have dreamed out whole years in lawless sheets   25
And secret incests, cursing one another.
Then you will wish each kiss your brother gave
Had been a dagger's point; then you shall hear
How he will cry, 'O would my wicked sister
Had first been damned, when she did yield to lust!'—   30
But soft, methinks I see repentance work
New motions in your heart; say, how is't with you?

ANNABELLA
Is there no way left to redeem my miseries?

FRIAR
There is, despair not; Heaven is merciful,
And offers grace even now. 'Tis thus agreed,   35

---

6 *read a lecture* deliver a reprimand (*O.E.D.* 6)

---

24 *There stands* etc. The Friar seems unable to depict a punishment
appropriate to incest. The usurer drinking gold is a common subject in
art and literature, but I know of no such image for the incestuous.
Dante would presumably have considered incest among the Sins against
Nature, but the incestuous have no place in the *Inferno*.

First, for your honour's safety, that you marry
The Lord Soranzo; next, to save your soul,
Leave off this life, and henceforth live to him.

ANNABELLA
Ay me!

FRIAR   Sigh not; I know the baits of sin
Are hard to leave. O, 'tis a death to do't.   40
Remember what must come. Are you content?

ANNABELLA
I am.

FRIAR   I like it well; we'll take the time.
Who's near us there?

                    Enter FLORIO *and* GIOVANNI

FLORIO
Did you call, father?

FRIAR
Is Lord Soranzo come?

FLORIO   He stays below.   45

FRIAR
Have you acquainted him at full?

FLORIO   I have,
And he is overjoyed.

FRIAR   And so are we.
Bid him come near.

GIOVANNI [*Aside*]   My sister weeping, ha?
I fear this friar's falsehood.—I will call him.   *Exit*

FLORIO
Daughter, are you resolved?

ANNABELLA   Father, I am.   50

            Enter GIOVANNI, SORANZO, *and* VASQUES

FLORIO
My Lord Soranzo, here
Give me your hand; for that I give you this.
                                [Joins their hands]

SORANZO
Lady, say you so too?

42 *take the time* seize the opportunity

51-6 *My Lord* etc. This is, strictly speaking, a betrothal not a marriage
    (see Ernest Schanzer, *The Problem Plays of Shakespeare*, 1963, 75-9).
    But such a betrothal would be legally binding, and would normally be
    followed by a church service as soon as possible. There is perhaps some
    slight discrepancy between III.vi, 55-6 and III.viii, 3-4.

ANNABELLA   I do, and vow
  To live with you and yours.
FRIAR   Timely resolved:
  My blessing rest on both; more to be done,   55
  You may perform it on the morning sun.   *Exeunt*

[Act III, Scene vii]

Enter GRIMALDI *with his rapier drawn and a dark lantern*

GRIMALDI
  'Tis early night as yet, and yet too soon
  To finish such a work; here I will lie
  To listen who comes next.   *He lies down*

    Enter BERGETTO *and* PHILOTIS *disguised, and after*
        RICHARDETTO *and* POGGIO

BERGETTO
  We are almost at the place, I hope, sweetheart.
GRIMALDI
  [*Aside*] I hear them near, and heard one say 'sweetheart'.   5
  'Tis he; now guide my hand, some angry justice,
  Home to his bosom.—Now have at you, sir!
          Strikes BERGETTO *and exit*
BERGETTO
  O help, help! Here's a stitch fallen in my guts. O for a
  flesh-tailor quickly!—Poggio!
PHILOTIS
  What ails my love?   10
BERGETTO
  I am sure I cannot piss forward and backward, and yet I
  am wet before and behind.—Lights, lights! ho, lights!
PHILOTIS
  Alas, some villain here has slain my love.
RICHARDETTO
  O Heaven forbid it.—Raise up the next neighbours
  Instantly, Poggio, and bring lights.   *Exit* POGGIO   15
  How is't, Bergetto? Slain? It cannot be;
  Are you sure y'are hurt?

---

9 *flesh-tailor* surgeon

---

1 s.d. *dark lantern.* A lantern with a slide or arrangement by which the light
  can be concealed.

BERGETTO

O my belly seethes like a porridge-pot; some cold water,
I shall boil over else; my whole body is in a sweat, that you
may wring my shirt; feel here—Why, Poggio!   20

Enter POGGIO *with* OFFICERS *and lights and halberts*

POGGIO

Here. Alas, how do you?

RICHARDETTO

Give me a light. What's here? All blood! O sirs,
Signor Donado's nephew now is slain.
Follow the murderer with all despatch
Up to the city, he cannot be far hence;   25
Follow, I beseech you.

OFFICERS

Follow, follow, follow.   *Exeunt* OFFICERS

RICHARDETTO

Tear off thy linen, coz, to stop his wounds.—
Be of good comfort, man.

BERGETTO

Is all this mine own blood? Nay then, good night with me.   30
Poggio, commend me to my uncle, dost hear? Bid him for
my sake make much of this wench. O!—I am going the
wrong way sure, my belly aches so.—O, farewell, Poggio!—
O!—O!—   *Dies*

PHILOTIS

O, he is dead.

POGGIO   How! Dead!

RICHARDETTO   He's dead indeed.   35
'Tis now too late to weep; let's have him home,
And with what speed we may, find out the murderer.

POGGIO

O my master, my master, my master!   *Exeunt*

[Act III, Scene viii]

Enter VASQUES *and* HIPPOLITA

HIPPOLITA

Betrothed?

VASQUES

I saw it.

---

24 *with all despatch.* Q reads 'with all the haste' but I cannot believe Ford
    wrote it. The two forms, written down, could look alike.

HIPPOLITA
  And when's the marriage-day?
VASQUES
  Some two days hence.
HIPPOLITA
  Two days? Why, man, I would but wish two hours   5
  To send him to his last, and lasting sleep.
  And, Vasques, thou shalt see I'll do it bravely.
VASQUES
  I do not doubt your wisdom, nor, I trust, you my secrecy;
  I am infinitely yours.
HIPPOLITA
  I will be thine in spite of my disgrace.   10
  So soon? O, wicked man, I durst be sworn,
  He'd laugh to see me weep.
VASQUES
  And that's a villainous fault in him.
HIPPOLITA
  No, let him laugh, I'm armed in my resolves;
  Be thou still true.   15
VASQUES
  I should get little by treachery against so hopeful a prefer-
  ment as I am like to climb to.
HIPPOLITA
  Even to my bosom, Vasques. Let my youth
  Revel in these new pleasures; if we thrive,
  He now hath but a pair of days to live.   *Exeunt*   20

[Act III, Scene ix]

Enter FLORIO, DONADO, RICHARDETTO, POGGIO *and*
                    OFFICERS

FLORIO
  'Tis bootless now to show yourself a child,
  Signor Donado; what is done, is done.
  Spend not the time in tears, but seek for justice.
RICHARDETTO
  I must confess, somewhat I was in fault
  That had not first acquainted you what love   5
  Passed 'twixt him and my niece; but, as I live,
  His fortune grieves me as it were mine own.

18 *my youth* Soranzo
  1 *bootless* pointless

DONADO
>   Alas, poor creature, he meant no man harm,
>   That I am sure of.

FLORIO   I believe that too.
>   But stay, my masters, are you sure you saw   10
>   The murderer pass here?

OFFICER
>   And it please you, sir, we are sure we saw a ruffian, with a
>   naked weapon in his hand all bloody, get into my lord
>   cardinal's grace's gate, that we are sure of; but for fear of
>   his grace (bless us) we durst go no further.   15

DONADO
>   Know you what manner of man he was?

OFFICER
>   Yes, sure, I know the man; they say 'a is a soldier; he that
>   loved your daughter, sir, an't please ye; 'twas he for certain.

FLORIO
>   Grimaldi, on my life.

OFFICER   Ay, ay, the same.

RICHARDETTO
>   The cardinal is noble; he no doubt   20
>   Will give true justice.

DONADO
>   Knock someone at the gate.

POGGIO
>   I'll knock, sir.   POGGIO *knocks*

SERVANT *within*
>   What would 'ee?

FLORIO
>   We require speech with the lord cardinal   25
>   About some present business; pray inform
>   His grace that we are here.

Enter CARDINAL *and* GRIMALDI

CARDINAL
>   Why, how now, friends! What saucy mates are you
>   That know nor duty nor civility?
>   Are we a person fit to be your host,   30
>   Or is our house become your common inn,
>   To beat our doors at pleasure? What such haste
>   Is yours as that it cannot wait fit times?
>   Are you the masters of this commonwealth,

17 *'a* he
26 *present* urgent

And know no more discretion? O, your news   35
Is here before you; you have lost a nephew,
Donado, last night by Grimaldi slain:
Is that your business? Well, sir, we have knowledge on't.
Let that suffice.

GRIMALDI   In presence of your grace,
In thought I never meant Bergetto harm.   40
But Florio, you can tell, with how much scorn
Soranzo, backed with his confederates,
Hath often wronged me; I, to be revenged,
(For that I could not win him else to fight)
Had thought by way of ambush to have killed him,   45
But was unluckily therein mistook;
Else he had felt what late Bergetto did:
And though my fault to him were merely chance,
Yet humbly I submit me to your grace,
To do with me as you please.

CARDINAL   Rise up, Grimaldi.   50
You citizens of Parma, if you seek
For justice, know, as nuncio from the Pope,
For this offence I here receive Grimaldi
Into his holiness' protection.
He is no common man, but nobly born;   55
Of princes' blood, though you, Sir Florio,
Thought him too mean a husband for your daughter.
If more you seek for, you must go to Rome,
For he shall thither; learn more wit, for shame.
Bury your dead.—Away, Grimaldi; leave 'em.   60

                    Exeunt CARDINAL *and* GRIMALDI

DONADO
Is this a churchman's voice? Dwells justice here?
FLORIO
Justice is fled to Heaven and comes no nearer.
Soranzo. Was't for him? O impudence.
Had he the face to speak it, and not blush?
Come, come, Donado, there's no help in this,   65
When cardinals think murder's not amiss.
Great men may do their wills, we must obey;
But Heaven will judge them for't another day.   *Exeunt*

---

62 *fled to Heaven.* Astraea, goddess of Justice, fled to Heaven at the end of
the Golden Age on earth. See Ovid, *Metamorphoses*, I, 149.

Act IV, [Scene i]

A Banquet. Hautboys. Enter the FRIAR, GIOVANNI, ANNABELLA,
PHILOTIS, SORANZO, DONADO, FLORIO, RICHARDETTO, PUTANA,
and VASQUES

FRIAR
These holy rites performed, now take your times
To spend the remnant of the day in feast;
Such fit repasts are pleasing to the saints,
Who are your guests, though not with mortal eyes
To be beheld.—Long prosper in this day,   5
You happy couple, to each other's joy.

SORANZO
Father, your prayer is heard; the hand of goodness
Hath been a shield for me against my death;
And, more to bless me, hath enriched my life
With this most precious jewel; such a prize   10
As earth hath not another like to this.
Cheer up, my love, and gentlemen, my friends,
Rejoice with me in mirth; this day we'll crown
With lusty cups to Annabella's health.

GIOVANNI
[*Aside*] O torture. Were the marriage yet undone,   15
Ere I'd endure this sight, to see my love
Clipped by another, I would dare confusion,
And stand the horror of ten thousand deaths.

VASQUES
Are you not well, sir?

GIOVANNI   Prithee, fellow, wait;
I need not thy officious diligence.   20

FLORIO
Signor Donado, come, you must forget
Your late mishaps, and drown your cares in wine.

SORANZO
Vasques.

VASQUES   My lord?

s.d. *Hautboys* Oboes
17 *Clipped* Embraced
19 *wait* wait on the guests

---

s.d. *A Banquet.* Bawcutt glosses 'a dessert of confectionery, fruit, wine, etc.'
This is possible (*O.E.D.* 3), but the Friar's words (1–6) and Soranzo's
reply suggest a more formal feast (*O.E.D.* 1). The question is important
in staging the play; cf. V.iii, 42–3, and V.vi, 1–6.

SORANZO   Reach me that weighty bowl.
  Here, brother Giovanni, here's to you;
  Your turn comes next, though now a bachelor.   25
  Here's to your sister's happiness and mine.
GIOVANNI
  I cannot drink.
SORANZO   What?
GIOVANNI   'Twill indeed offend me.
ANNABELLA
  Pray do not urge him, if he be not willing.   *Hautboys*
FLORIO
  How now, what noise is this?
VASQUES
  O, sir, I had forgot to tell you; certain young maidens of   30
  Parma, in honour to Madam Annabella's marriage, have
  sent their loves to her in a masque, for which they humbly
  crave your patience and silence.
SORANZO
  We are much bound to them, so much the more
  As it comes unexpected; guide them in.   35

    Enter HIPPOLITA *and Ladies in* [*masks and*] *white robes,*
      with garlands of willows. Music and a dance

  Thanks, lovely virgins; now might we but know
  To whom we have been beholding for this love,
  We shall acknowledge it.
HIPPOLITA   Yes, you shall know;   [*Unmasks*]
  What think you now?
OMNES   Hippolita!
HIPPOLITA   'Tis she,
  Be not amazed; nor blush, young lovely bride,   40
  I come not to defraud you of your man.
  'Tis now no time to reckon up the talk
  What Parma long hath rumoured of us both:
  Let rash report run on; the breath that vents it
  Will, like a bubble, break itself at last.   45

28 s.d. *Hautboys* ed.; after line 35 in Q
29 *noise* music (*O.E.D.* 5)
34 *bound* obliged
35 s.d. *a dance* ed.; a Daunce. Dance Q
37 *this* Q *a.c.*; thy Q *b.c.*

---

35 s.d. *willows*. Symbol of disappointed love. Cf. *The Merchant of Venice*,
  V.i, 10 and *Othello*, IV.iii.

But now to you, sweet creature: lend's your hand;
Perhaps it hath been said that I would claim
Some interest in Soranzo, now your lord.
What I have right to do, his soul knows best;
But in my duty to your noble worth,   50
Sweet Annabella, and my care of you,
Here take, Soranzo, take this hand from me:
I'll once more join what by the holy church
Is finished and allowed. Have I done well?

SORANZO
You have too much engaged us.

HIPPOLITA   One thing more.   55
That you may know my single charity,
Freely I here remit all interest
I e'er could claim, and give you back your vows;
And to confirm't—reach me a cup of wine—
My Lord Soranzo, in this draught I drink   60
Long rest t'ee.—Look to it, Vasques.

VASQUES
Fear nothing.   *He gives her a poisoned cup: she drinks*

SORANZO
Hippolita, I thank you, and will pledge
This happy union as another life;
Wine, there!   65

VASQUES
You shall have none, neither shall you pledge her.

HIPPOLITA
How!

VASQUES
Know now, Mistress She-Devil, your own mischievous
treachery hath killed you; I must not marry you.

HIPPOLITA
Villain.   70

OMNES
What's the matter?

VASQUES
Foolish woman, thou art now like a firebrand that hath
kindled others and burnt thyself; *troppo sperar, inganna,*

55 *engaged* placed under obligation
56 *single* signal, outstanding
56 *charity* love
73 *inganna* ed. niganna Q

---

73 *troppo . . . inganna.* Too much hope deceives.

thy vain hope hath deceived thee, thou art but dead; if
thou hast any grace, pray.   75

HIPPOLITA
Monster.

VASQUES
Die in charity, for shame.—This thing of malice, this
woman, had privately corrupted me with promise of
marriage, under this politic reconciliation, to poison my
lord, whiles she might laugh at his confusion on his marriage   80
day. I promised her fair, but I knew what my reward
should have been; and would willingly have spared her
life, but that I was acquainted with the danger of her
disposition, and now have fitted her a just payment in her
own coin. There she is, she hath yet—and end thy days in   85
peace, vile woman; as for life there's no hope, think not on't.

OMNES
Wonderful justice!

RICHARDETTO   Heaven, thou art righteous.

HIPPOLITA
O, 'tis true;
I feel my minute coming. Had that slave
Kept promise (O, my torment) thou this hour   90
Hadst died, Soranzo—heat above hell fire—
Yet ere I pass away—cruel, cruel flames—
Take here my curse amongst you: may thy bed
Of marriage be a rack unto thy heart,
Burn blood and boil in vengeance—O my heart,   95
My flame's intolerable—Mayst thou live
To father bastards, may her womb bring forth
Monsters, and die together in your sins,
Hated, scorned, and unpitied—O!—O!—   *Dies*

FLORIO
Was e'er so vile a creature?

RICHARDETTO   Here's the end   100
Of lust and pride.

ANNABELLA   It is a fearful sight.

---

79 *marriage* ed. malice Q
79 *politic reconciliation* cunning agreement

---

85 *yet—and.* The manuscript was either incomplete or illegible at this
point, and some words are missing. The hiatus need be no longer than a
line; to bridge the sense we need only phrases like 'a moment to live.
Pray, then'.

SORANZO
  Vasques, I know thee now a trusty servant,
  And never will forget thee.——Come, my love,
  We'll home, and thank the Heavens for this escape.
  Father and friends, we must break up this mirth;   105
  It is too sad a feast.

DONADO   Bear hence the body.

FRIAR
  Here's an ominous change;
  Mark this, my Giovanni, and take heed.
  I fear the event; that marriage seldom's good,
  Where the bride-banquet so begins in blood.   *Exeunt*   110

[Act IV, Scene ii]

Enter RICHARDETTO *and* PHILOTIS

RICHARDETTO
  My wretched wife, more wretched in her shame
  Than in her wrongs to me, hath paid too soon
  The forfeit of her modesty and life;
  And I am sure, my niece, though vengeance hover,
  Keeping aloof yet from Soranzo's fall,   5
  Yet he will fall, and sink with his own weight.
  I need not now—my heart persuades me so—
  To further his confusion; there is One
  Above begins to work, for, as I hear,
  Debates already 'twixt his wife and him   10
  Thicken and run to head; she, as 'tis said,
  Slightens his love, and he abandons hers.
  Much talk I hear. Since things go thus, my niece,
  In tender love and pity of your youth,
  My counsel is, that you should free your years   15
  From hazard of these woes by flying hence
  To fair Cremona, there to vow your soul
  In holiness a holy votaress:

109 *event* outcome
2 *hath* Q *a.c.*; hath hath Q *b.c.*
10 *Debates* Quarrels, arguments
12 *Slightens* Disdains

---

11 *Thicken and run to head.* Come to maturation point, like a ripe boil
ready to burst.
18 *In holiness* etc. The repetition in this line is weak, and unlike Ford's
style. He may have written 'a godly votaress', the two forms being
similar in seventeenth-century handwriting.

Leave me to see the end of these extremes.
All human worldly courses are uneven;   20
No life is blessed but the way to Heaven.

PHILOTIS
Uncle, shall I resolve to be a nun?

RICHARDETTO
Ay, gentle niece, and in your hourly prayers
Remember me, your poor unhappy uncle.
Hie to Cremona now, as fortune leads,   25
Your home your cloister, your best friends your beads.
Your chaste and single life shall crown your birth;
Who dies a virgin lives a saint on earth.

PHILOTIS
Then farewell, world, and worldly thoughts, adieu.
Welcome, chaste vows; myself I yield to you.   *Exeunt*   30

[Act IV, Scene iii]

Enter SORANZO *unbraced, and* ANNABELLA *dragged in*

SORANZO
Come, strumpet, famous whore! Were every drop
Of blood that runs in thy adulterous veins
A life, this sword (dost see't?) should in one blow
Confound them all. Harlot, rare, notable harlot,
That with thy brazen face maintainst thy sin,   5
Was there no man in Parma to be bawd
To your loose cunning whoredom else but I?
Must your hot itch and pleurisy of lust,
The heyday of your luxury, be fed
Up to a surfeit, and could none but I   10
Be picked out to be cloak to your close tricks,
Your belly-sports? Now I must be the dad
To all that gallimaufry that's stuffed
In thy corrupted bastard-bearing womb,
Say, must I?

ANNABELLA   Beastly man! Why, 'tis thy fate.   15
I sued not to thee; for, but that I thought

28 *lives* ed. live Q
s.d. *unbraced* cf. *Hamlet*, II.i, 78
  8 *pleurisy* superabundance, excess (*O.E.D.* 2)
  9 *heyday of your luxury* height of your lechery
 11 *close* secret
 13 *gallimaufry* mixture, hodge-podge
 15 *Say* ed. Shey Q

Your over-loving lordship would have run
Mad on denial, had ye lent me time,
I would have told 'ee in what case I was.
But you would needs be doing.
SORANZO   Whore of whores!   20
Dar'st thou tell me this?
ANNABELLA   O yes, why not?
You were deceived in me; 'twas not for love
I chose you, but for honour; yet know this,
Would you be patient yet, and hide your shame,
I'd see whether I could love you.
SORANZO   Excellent quean!   25
Why, art thou not with child?
ANNABELLA   What needs all this
When 'tis superfluous? I confess I am.
SORANZO
Tell me by whom.
ANNABELLA   Soft, sir, 'twas not in my bargain.
Yet somewhat, sir, to stay your longing stomach,
I am content t'acquaint you with; the man,   30
The more than man, that got this sprightly boy—
For 'tis a boy, and therefore glory, sir,
Your heir shall be a son—
SORANZO   Damnable monster!
ANNABELLA
Nay, and you will not hear, I'll speak no more.
SORANZO
Yes, speak, and speak thy last.
ANNABELLA   A match, a match!   35
This noble creature was in every part
So angel-like, so glorious, that a woman
Who had not been but human, as was I,
Would have kneeled to him, and have begged for love.
You! Why, you are not worthy once to name   40
His name without true worship, or, indeed,
Unless you kneeled, to hear another name him.
SORANZO
What was he called?
ANNABELLA   We are not come to that.
Let it suffice that you shall have the glory
To father what so brave a father got.   45

25 *quean* whore
30 *I am* ed. I'me Q
32 *and therefore* ed. that for Q

In brief, had not this chance fallen out as't doth,
I never had been troubled with a thought
That you had been a creature; but for marriage,
I scarce dream yet of that.
SORANZO
Tell me his name.
ANNABELLA   Alas, alas, there's all.   50
Will you believe?
SORANZO   What?
ANNABELLA   You shall never know.
SORANZO
How!
ANNABELLA   Never; if you do, let me be cursed.
SORANZO
Not know it, strumpet? I'll rip up thy heart,
And find it there.
ANNABELLA   Do, do.
SORANZO   And with my teeth
Tear the prodigious lecher joint by joint.   55
ANNABELLA
Ha, ha, ha, the man's merry!
SORANZO   Dost thou laugh?
Come, whore, tell me your lover, or, by truth,
I'll hew thy flesh to shreds; who is't?
ANNABELLA *sings*
Che morte piu dolce che morire per amore?
SORANZO
Thus will I pull thy hair, and thus I'll drag   60
Thy lust-be-lepered body through the dust.
Yet tell his name.
ANNABELLA *sings*
Morendo in gratia Dei, morirei senza dolore.
SORANZO
Dost thou triumph? The treasure of the earth

59 *piu* ed. pluis Q   63 *Dei* ed. Lei Q
63 *morirei* ed. morirere Q *a.c.*; *morire* Q *b.c.*

---

59 *Che morte* etc. 'What death is sweeter than to die for love.'
63 *Morendo in gratia* etc. 'Dying in the grace of God, I should die without
   sorrow.' Bawcutt's emendation 'morirei' for the corrected Q reading
   'Morirere' is admirable; a compositor ignorant of Italian might easily
   misread this word twice—in an italic or mixed hand it is little more than
   a row of minims. No editor has identified Annabella's songs; nothing
   like them is listed in Einstein's *The Italian Madrigal*, Princeton, 1949.

Shall not redeem thee; were there kneeling kings   65
Did beg thy life, or angels did come down
To plead in tears, yet should not all prevail
Against my rage. Dost thou not tremble yet?

ANNABELLA
At what? To die? No, be a gallant hangman.
I dare thee to the worst: strike, and strike home;   70
I leave revenge behind, and thou shalt feel't.

SORANZO
Yet tell me ere thou diest, and tell me truly,
Knows thy old father this?

ANNABELLA   No, by my life.

SORANZO
Wilt thou confess, and I will spare thy life?

ANNABELLA
My life? I will not buy my life so dear.   75

SORANZO
I will not slack my vengeance.

Enter VASQUES

VASQUES
What d'ee mean, sir?

SORANZO
Forbear, Vasques; such a damned whore
Deserves no pity.

VASQUES
Now the gods forfend! And would you be her executioner,   80
and kill her in your rage too? O, 'twere most unmanlike.
She is your wife: what faults hath been done by her before
she married you, were not against you; alas, poor lady, what
hath she committed which any lady in Italy in the like case
would not? Sir, you must be ruled by your reason and not   85
by your fury; that were unhuman and beastly.

SORANZO
She shall not live.

VASQUES
Come, she must. You would have her confess the author
of her present misfortunes, I warrant 'ee; 'tis an unconscion-
able demand, and she should lose the estimation that I,   90

---

69 *hangman* general term for executioner
71 *I leave* Q *a.c.*; *leave* Q *b.c.*
76 *slack* reduce, mitigate
80 *forfend* forbid
88 *author* ed. Authors Q

for my part, hold of her worth, if she had done it. Why,
sir, you ought not of all men living to know it. Good sir,
be reconciled; alas, good gentlewoman.

ANNABELLA
Pish, do not beg for me; I prize my life
As nothing; if the man will needs be mad,   95
Why, let him take it.

SORANZO   Vasques, hear'st thou this?

VASQUES
Yes, and commend her for it; in this she shows the nobleness
of a gallant spirit, and beshrew my heart, but it becomes her
rarely. [*Aside*] Sir, in any case smother your revenge;
leave the scenting-out your wrongs to me; be ruled, as you   100
respect your honour, or you mar all. [*Aloud*] Sir, if ever
my service were of any credit with you, be not so violent
in your distractions. You are married now; what a triumph
might the report of this give to other neglected suitors. 'Tis
as manlike to bear extremities as godlike to forgive.   105

SORANZO
O Vasques, Vasques, in this piece of flesh,
This faithless face of hers, had I laid up
The treasure of my heart.—Hadst thou been virtuous,
Fair, wicked woman, not the matchless joys
Of life itself had made me wish to live   110
With any saint but thee; deceitful creature,
How hast thou mocked my hopes, and in the shame
Of thy lewd womb even buried me alive.
I did too dearly love thee.

VASQUES
[*Aside*] This is well; follow this temper with some passion.   115
Be brief and moving; 'tis for the purpose.

SORANZO
Be witness to my words thy soul and thoughts,
And tell me, didst not think that in my heart
I did too superstitiously adore thee?

ANNABELLA
I must confess I know you loved me well.   120

SORANZO
And wouldst thou use me thus? O, Annabella,
Be thou assured, whatsoe'er the villain was

99 *in any case* by any means (*O.E.D.* 13)
101 *your* ed. hour Q
115 *temper* state of mind
122 *thou* ed. thus Q

That thus hath tempted thee to this disgrace,
Well he might lust, but never loved like me.
He doted on the picture that hung out   125
Upon thy cheeks, to please his humorous eye;
Not on the part I loved, which was thy heart,
And, as I thought, thy virtues.

ANNABELLA   O my lord!
These words wound deeper than your sword could do.

VASQUES
Let me not ever take comfort, but I begin to weep myself,   130
so much I pity him; why, madam, I knew when his rage was
over-past, what it would come to.

SORANZO
Forgive me, Annabella. Though thy youth
Hath tempted thee above thy strength to folly,
Yet will not I forget what I should be,   135
And what I am, a husband; in that name
Is hid divinity; if I do find
That thou wilt yet be true, here I remit
All former faults, and take thee to my bosom.

VASQUES
By my troth, and that's a point of noble charity.   140

ANNABELLA
Sir, on my knees—

SORANZO   Rise up, you shall not kneel.
Get you to your chamber, see you make no show
Of alteration; I'll be with you straight.
My reason tells me now that 'tis as common
To err in frailty as to be a woman.   145
Go to your chamber.   *Exit* ANNABELLA

VASQUES
So, this was somewhat to the matter; what do you think
of your heaven of happiness now, sir?

SORANZO
I carry hell about me; all my blood
Is fired in swift revenge.   150

VASQUES
That may be, but know you how, or on whom? Alas, to
marry a great woman, being made great in the stock to
your hand, is a usual sport in these days; but to know what

126 *humorous* whimsical
152 *great* pregnant
152 *stock* trunk, body
152–3 *to your hand* ready for you

ferret it was that haunted your cony-berry, there's the
cunning.   155

SORANZO

I'll make her tell herself, or—

VASQUES

Or what? You must not do so. Let me yet persuade your
sufferance a little while; go to her, use her mildly, win her
if it be possible to a voluntary, to a weeping tune; for the
rest, if all hit, I will not miss my mark. Pray, sir, go in; the   160
next news I tell you shall be wonders.

SORANZO

Delay in vengeance gives a heavier blow.   *Exit*

VASQUES

Ah, sirrah, here's work for the nonce. I had a suspicion of
a bad matter in my head a pretty whiles ago; but after my
madam's scurvy looks here at home, her waspish perver-   165
seness and loud fault-finding, then I remembered the
proverb, that where hens crow and cocks hold their peace
there are sorry houses. 'Sfoot, if the lower parts of a she-
tailor's cunning can cover such a swelling in the stomach,
I'll never blame a false stitch in a shoe whiles I live again.   170
Up and up so quick? And so quickly too? 'Twere a fine
policy to learn by whom; this must be known; and I have
thought on't—

                        Enter PUTANA

Here's the way, or none—What, crying, old mistress! Alas,
alas, I cannot blame 'ee, we have a lord, Heaven help us, is so   175
mad as the devil himself, the more shame for him.

PUTANA

O Vasques, that ever I was born to see this day. Doth he
use thee so too, sometimes, Vasques?

VASQUES

Me? Why, he makes a dog of me. But if some were of my
mind, I know what we would do; as sure as I am an honest   180
man, he will go near to kill my lady with unkindness. Say

---

154 *ferret* ed. secret Q
154 *cony-berry* rabbit-warren
155 *cunning* skill
173 s.d. ed.; after line 176 in Q

---

159 *voluntary*. Meaning, here, both 'an improvised piece of music' and 'a
    spontaneous confession'.
167–8 *where . . . houses*. Proverbial. See Tilley, H778.

she be with child, is that such a matter for a young woman
of her years to be blamed for?

PUTANA

Alas, good heart, it is against her will full sore.

VASQUES

I durst be sworn, all his madness is for that she will not   185
confess whose 'tis, which he will know, and when he doth
know it, I am so well acquainted with his humour, that he
will forget all straight. Well, I could wish she would in plain
terms tell all, for that's the way indeed.

PUTANA

Do you think so?   190

VASQUES

Foh, I know't; provided that he did not win her to't by
force. He was once in a mind that you could tell, and meant
to have wrung it out of you, but I somewhat pacified him
for that; yet sure you know a great deal.

PUTANA

Heaven forgive us all! I know a little, Vasques.   195

VASQUES

Why should you not? Who else should? Upon my conscience, she loves you dearly, and you would not betray her
to any affliction for the world.

PUTANA

Not for all the world, by my faith and troth, Vasques.

VASQUES

'Twere pity of your life if you should; but in this you should   200
both relieve her present discomforts, pacify my lord, and
gain yourself everlasting love and preferment.

PUTANA

Dost think so, Vasques?

VASQUES

Nay, I know't; sure 'twas some near and entire friend.

PUTANA

'Twas a dear friend indeed; but—   205

VASQUES

But what? Fear not to name him; my life between you and
danger. Faith, I think 'twas no base fellow.

PUTANA

Thou wilt stand between me and harm?

VASQUES

'Ud's pity, what else? You shall be rewarded too, trust me.

209 *'Ud's* God's

PUTANA

'Twas even no worse than her own brother. 210

VASQUES

Her brother Giovanni, I warrant 'ee!

PUTANA

Even he, Vasques; as brave a gentleman as ever kissed fair
lady. O, they love most perpetually.

VASQUES

A brave gentleman indeed; why, therein I commend her
choice.—Better and better!—You are sure 'twas he? 215

PUTANA

Sure; and you shall see he will not be long from her too.

VASQUES

He were to blame if he would: but may I believe thee?

PUTANA

Believe me! Why, dost think I am a Turk or a Jew? No,
Vasques, I have known their dealings too long to belie them
now. 220

VASQUES

Where are you? There within, sirs.

Enter BANDITTI

PUTANA

How now, what are these?

VASQUES

You shall know presently. Come, sirs, take me this old
damnable hag, gag her instantly, and put out her eyes.
Quickly, quickly! 225

PUTANA

Vasques, Vasques!

VASQUES

Gag her, I say. 'Sfoot, d'ee suffer her to prate? What d'ee
fumble about? Let me come to her; I'll help your old
gums, you toad-bellied bitch. Sirs, carry her closely into the
coalhouse, and put out her eyes instantly; if she roars, slit 230
her nose: d'ee hear, be speedy and sure. Why, this is
excellent and above expectation.

Exeunt [BANDITTI] *with* PUTANA

Her own brother! O horrible! To what a height of liberty
in damnation hath the devil trained our age. Her brother!

223 *presently* at once
232 s.d. *Exeunt* ed. Exit Q
233 *liberty* licence
234 *trained* lured

Well, there's yet but a beginning: I must to my lord, and 235
tutor him better in his points of vengeance; now I see
how a smooth tale goes beyond a smooth tail. But soft—
What thing comes next?

Enter GIOVANNI

Giovanni! As I would wish; my belief is strengthened,
'tis as firm as winter and summer.   240

GIOVANNI

Where's my sister?

VASQUES

Troubled with a new sickness, my lord; she's somewhat
ill.

GIOVANNI

Took too much of the flesh, I believe.

VASQUES

Troth, sir, and you, I think, have e'en hit it. But my virtuous 245
lady—

GIOVANNI

Where's she?

VASQUES

In her chamber; please you visit her; she is alone. [GIOVANNI
gives him money] Your liberality hath doubly made me
your servant, and ever shall, ever.   *Exit* GIOVANNI 250

Enter SORANZO

Sir, I am made a man, I have plied my cue with cunning
and success; I beseech you let's be private.

SORANZO

My lady's brother's come; now he'll know all.

VASQUES

Let him know't; I have made some of them fast enough.
How have you dealt with my lady?   255

SORANZO

Gently, as thou hast counselled. O, my soul
Runs circular in sorrow for revenge.
But, Vasques, thou shalt know—

VASQUES

Nay, I will know no more, for now comes your turn to
know; I would not talk so openly with you. Let my young 260

---

244 *Took . . . flesh*. Meaning both 'eaten too much meat' and 'had too much
    sexual experience'.
249 *liberality*. Both 'generosity' and 'sexual licence'.

master take time enough, and go at pleasure; he is sold to
death, and the devil shall not ransom him. Sir, I beseech
you, your privacy.

SORANZO

No conquest can gain glory of my fear.   *Exeunt*

Act V, [Scene i]

Enter ANNABELLA *above*

ANNABELLA

Pleasures, farewell, and all ye thriftless minutes
Wherein false joys have spun a weary life.
To these my fortunes now I take my leave.
Thou, precious Time, that swiftly rid'st in post
Over the world, to finish up the race   5
Of my last fate, here stay thy restless course,
And bear to ages that are yet unborn
A wretched, woeful woman's tragedy.
My conscience now stands up against my lust
With depositions charactered in guilt,   10

Enter FRIAR [*below*]

And tells me I am lost: now I confess
Beauty that clothes the outside of the face
Is cursèd if it be not clothed with grace.
Here like a turtle (mewed up in a cage)
Unmated, I converse with air and walls,   15
And descant on my vile unhappiness.
O Giovanni, that hast had the spoil
Of thine own virtues and my modest fame,
Would thou hadst been less subject to those stars
That luckless reigned at my nativity: 20

264 s.d. *Exeunt* ed. Exit Q
  9 *against* to witness against
 10 *depositions* ed. dispositions Q
 14 *turtle* turtle-dove
 14 *mewed up* imprisoned

---

  4 *rid'st in post.* With post horses, express, with haste (*O.E.D.*, adv.). The
    phrase may also carry something of the meaning 'in stages.'
 10 *charactered in guilt.* Bawcutt points out the pun: (1) with gilt lettering;
    (2) written so as to expose Annabella's guilt. Unlike the puns at the end
    of IV.iii, this one would not be easy to make on stage.
12–13 *Beauty . . . grace.* Cf. II.v, 15ff., and see Tilley, B175.

O would the scourge due to my black offence
Might pass from thee, that I alone might feel
The torment of an uncontrolled flame.
FRIAR
[*Aside*] What's this I hear?
ANNABELLA   That man, that blessed friar,
Who joined in ceremonial knot my hand   25
To him whose wife I now am, told me oft
I trod the path to death, and showed me how.
But they who sleep in lethargies of lust
Hug their confusion, making Heaven unjust,
And so did I.
FRIAR [*Aside*]   Here's music to the soul.   30
ANNABELLA
Forgive me, my good genius, and this once
Be helpful to my ends. Let some good man
Pass this way, to whose trust I may commit
This paper double-lined with tears and blood:
Which being granted, here I sadly vow   35
Repentance, and a leaving of that life
I long have died in.
FRIAR   Lady, Heaven hath heard you,
And hath by providence ordained that I
Should be his minister for your behoof.
ANNABELLA
Ha, what are you?
FRIAR   Your brother's friend, the friar;   40
Glad in my soul that I have lived to hear
This free confession 'twixt your peace and you.
What would you, or to whom? Fear not to speak.
ANNABELLA
Is Heaven so bountiful? Then I have found
More favour than I hoped. Here, holy man—   45
                              Throws a letter
Commend me to my brother; give him that,
That letter; bid him read it and repent.
Tell him that I (imprisoned in my chamber,
Barred of all company, even of my guardian,
Who gives me cause of much suspect) have time   50
To blush at what hath passed; bid him be wise,
And not believe the friendship of my lord.

35 *sadly* solemnly
39 *behoof* advantage
50 *suspect* suspicion

I fear much more than I can speak: good father,
The place is dangerous, and spies are busy;
I must break off—you'll do't?

FRIAR   Be sure I will;   55
And fly with speed—my blessing ever rest
With thee, my daughter; live, to die more blessed.

Exit FRIAR

ANNABELLA
  Thanks to the Heavens, who have prolonged my breath
  To this good use: now I can welcome death.   *Exit*

[Act V, Scene ii]

Enter SORANZO *and* VASQUES

VASQUES
  Am I to be believed now? First marry a strumpet that cast
  herself away upon you but to laugh at your horns, to feast
  on your disgrace, riot in your vexations, cuckold you in your
  bride-bed, waste your estate upon panders and bawds!

SORANZO
  No more, I say, no more.   5

VASQUES
  A cuckold is a goodly tame beast, my lord.

SORANZO
  I am resolved; urge not another word.
  My thoughts are great, and all as resolute
  As thunder; in mean time I'll cause our lady
  To deck herself in all her bridal robes,   10
  Kiss her, and fold her gently in my arms.
  Begone—yet hear you, are the banditti ready
  To wait in ambush?

VASQUES
  Good sir, trouble not yourself about other business than
  your own resolution; remember that time lost cannot be   15
  recalled.

SORANZO
  With all the cunning words thou canst, invite
  The states of Parma to my birthday's feast;
  Haste to my brother-rival and his father,
  Entreat them gently, bid them not to fail.   20
  Be speedy, and return.

18 *states* nobles

15–16 *time lost* etc. Tilley, T332.

VASQUES

Let not your pity betray you till my coming back; think upon
incest and cuckoldry.

SORANZO

Revenge is all the ambition I aspire:
To that I'll climb or fall; my blood's on fire.   *Exeunt*   25

[Act V, Scene iii]

Enter GIOVANNI

GIOVANNI

Busy opinion is an idle fool,
That, as a school-rod keeps a child in awe,
Frights the unexperienced temper of the mind:
So did it me; who, ere my precious sister
Was married, thought all taste of love would die   5
In such a contract; but I find no change
Of pleasure in this formal law of sports.
She is still one to me, and every kiss
As sweet and as delicious as the first
I reaped, when yet the privilege of youth   10
Entitled her a virgin. O the glory
Of two united hearts like hers and mine!
Let poring book-men dream of other worlds,
My world, and all of happiness, is here,
And I'd not change it for the best to come: 15
A life of pleasure is Elysium.

Enter FRIAR

Father, you enter on the jubilee
Of my retired delights; now I can tell you,
The hell you oft have prompted is nought else
But slavish and fond superstitious fear;   20
And I could prove it too—

FRIAR   Thy blindness slays thee.
Look there, 'tis writ to thee.   *Gives the letter*

GIOVANNI

From whom?

19 *prompted* put forward in argument
20 *fond* foolish

17 *jubilee*. Meaning not clear. It usually means 'a time of celebration')·
'the fiftieth anniversary.'

FRIAR

    Unrip the seals and see;

    The blood's yet seething hot, that will anon   25

    Be frozen harder than congealed coral.

    Why d'ee change colour, son?

GIOVANNI   'Fore Heaven, you make

    Some petty devil factor 'twixt my love

    And your religion-masked sorceries.

    Where had you this?

FRIAR   Thy conscience, youth, is seared,   30

    Else thou wouldst stoop to warning.

GIOVANNI   'Tis her hand,

    I know't; and 'tis all written in her blood.

    She writes I know not what. Death? I'll not fear

    An armèd thunderbolt aimed at my heart.

    She writes, we are discovered—pox on dreams   35

    Of low faint-hearted cowardice! Discovered?

    The devil we are; which way is't possible?

    Are we grown traitors to our own delights?

    Confusion take such dotage, 'tis but forged;

    This is your peevish chattering, weak old man.   40

Enter VASQUES

    Now, sir, what news bring you?

VASQUES

    My lord, according to his yearly custom keeping this day a

    feast in honour of his birthday, by me invites you thither.

    Your worthy father, with the Pope's reverend nuncio, and

    other magnificoes of Parma, have promised their presence;   45

    will't please you to be of the number?

GIOVANNI

    Yes, tell him I dare come.

VASQUES

    'Dare come'?

GIOVANNI

    So I said; and tell him more, I will come.

VASQUES

    These words are strange to me.   50

GIOVANNI

    Say I will come.

30 *seared* dried up

40 s.d. ed.; after line 41 in Q

47 *him* ed. them Q

VASQUES
  You will not miss?
GIOVANNI
  Yet more? I'll come! Sir, are you answered?
VASQUES
  So I'll say.—My service to you.   *Exit* VASQUES
FRIAR
  You will not go, I trust.
GIOVANNI   Not go? For what?   55
FRIAR
  O, do not go. This feast, I'll gage my life,
  Is but a plot to train you to your ruin.
  Be ruled, you sha' not go.
GIOVANNI   Not go? Stood Death
  Threatening his armies of confounding plagues,
  With hosts of dangers hot as blazing stars,   60
  I would be there. Not go? Yes, and resolve
  To strike as deep in slaughter as they all.
  For I will go.
FRIAR   Go where thou wilt; I see
  The wildness of thy fate draws to an end,
  To a bad fearful end. I must not stay   65
  To know thy fall; back to Bononia I
  With speed will haste, and shun this coming blow.
  Parma, farewell; would I had never known thee,
  Or aught of thine. Well, young man, since no prayer
  Can make thee safe, I leave thee to despair.   *Exit* FRIAR   70
GIOVANNI
  Despair, or tortures of a thousand hells,
  All's one to me; I have set up my rest.
  Now, now, work serious thoughts on baneful plots,
  Be all a man, my soul; let not the curse

56 *gage* wager   57 *train* lure
71 s.p. GIOVANNI ed.; omitted by Q

---

66 *back to Bononia.* Cf. *The Broken Heart* IV.i, where, as the tension
   increases, Tecnicus abandons Sparta for Delphos. In each play, when
   the hero is finally fixed in his course of action, the 'adviser' withdraws
   from the impending disaster.
72 *set up my rest.* Made up my mind. In the card-game Primero the
   player 'sets up his rest' when he 'stands' on the cards he has, and so
   ventures his all on them (*O.E.D.* Rest sb²7c).
74–5 *the curse . . . prescription.* The curse pronounced, in the Old
   Testament, upon him who lay with his sister. See Deuteronomy, xxvii,
   22, and Leviticus, xx, 17.

Of old prescription rend from me the gall   75
Of courage, which enrols a glorious death.
If I must totter like a well-grown oak,
Some under-shrubs shall in my weighty fall
Be crushed to splits: with me they all shall perish.   *Exit*

[Act V, Scene iv]

Enter SORANZO, VASQUES, *and* BANDITTI

SORANZO
You will not fail, or shrink in the attempt?

VASQUES
I will undertake for their parts. Be sure, my masters, to be
bloody enough, and as unmerciful as if you were preying
upon a rich booty on the very mountains of Liguria; for
your pardons, trust to my lord, but for reward you shall   5
trust none but your own pockets.

BANDITTI OMNES
We'll make a murder.

SORANZO
Here's gold, here's more; want nothing; what you do
Is noble, and an act of brave revenge.
I'll make ye rich banditti, and all free.   10

OMNES
Liberty, liberty!

VASQUES
Hold, take every man a vizard; when ye are withdrawn,
keep as much silence as you can possibly. You know the
watchword; till which be spoken, move not, but when you
hear that, rush in like a stormy flood; I need not instruct   15
ye in your own profession.

OMNES
No, no, no.

VASQUES
In, then; your ends are profit and preferment.—Away!
                              Exeunt BANDITTI

SORANZO
The guests will all come, Vasques?

VASQUES
Yes, sir. And now let me a little edge your resolution. You   20
see nothing is unready to this great work, but a great mind

75 *rend* ed. rent Q
79 *splits* splinters
18 s.d. *Exeunt* ed. Exit Q

in you: call to your remembrance your disgraces, your
loss of honour, Hippolita's blood, and arm your courage in
your own wrongs; so shall you best right those wrongs in
vengeance, which you may truly call your own.   25

SORANZO
'Tis well; the less I speak, the more I burn,
And blood shall quench that flame.

VASQUES
Now you begin to turn Italian. This beside—when my
young incest-monger comes, he will be sharp set on his old
bit: give him time enough, let him have your chamber and   30
bed at liberty; let my hot hare have law ere he be hunted
to his death, that if it be possible, he may post to hell in
the very act of his damnation.

Enter GIOVANNI

SORANZO
It shall be so; and see, as we would wish,
He comes himself first. Welcome, my much-loved brother,   35
Now I perceive you honour me; y'are welcome.
But where's my father?

GIOVANNI   With the other states,
Attending on the nuncio of the Pope,
To wait upon him hither. How's my sister?

SORANZO
Like a good housewife, scarcely ready yet;   40
Y'are best walk to her chamber.

GIOVANNI   If you will.

SORANZO
I must expect my honourable friends;
Good brother, get her forth.

GIOVANNI   You are busy, sir.

                                        Exit GIOVANNI

VASQUES
Even as the great devil himself would have it; let him go
and glut himself in his own destruction.   *Flourish*   45

42 *expect* wait for

29–30 *sharp set on his old bit*. Meaning 'eager', 'hungry for', but I have not
     been able to trace the metaphor further.
31 *law*. The 'start' which a hare is given before the chase begins.
32 *post to hell* etc. If he is killed while committing a sin his soul will go
     straight to hell. Cf. *Hamlet*, III.iii.
45 s.d. *Flourish*. The corrector of Q mistakenly placed this direction after
     line 47.

Hark, the nuncio is at hand; good sir, be ready to receive
him.

Enter CARDINAL, FLORIO, DONADO, RICHARDETTO, *and Attendants*

SORANZO
Most reverend lord, this grace hath made me proud,
That you vouchsafe my house; I ever rest
Your humble servant for this noble favour.   50
CARDINAL
You are our friend, my lord; his holiness
Shall understand how zealously you honour
Saint Peter's vicar in his substitute:
Our special love to you.
SORANZO   Signors, to you
My welcome, and my ever best of thanks   55
For this so memorable courtesy.
Pleaseth your grace to walk near?
CARDINAL   My lord, we come
To celebrate your feast with civil mirth,
As ancient custom teacheth: we will go.
SORANZO
Attend his grace there!—Signors, keep your way.   *Exeunt*   60

[Act V, Scene v]

Enter GIOVANNI *and* ANNABELLA *lying on a bed*
GIOVANNI
What, changed so soon? Hath your new sprightly lord
Found out a trick in night-games more than we
Could know in our simplicity? Ha! Is't so?
Or does the fit come on you, to prove treacherous
To your past vows and oaths?
ANNABELLA   Why should you jest   5
At my calamity, without all sense
Of the approaching dangers you are in?
GIOVANNI
What danger's half so great as thy revolt?
Thou art a faithless sister, else thou know'st

---

49 *vouchsafe* deign (to visit)

---

1 s.d. They may have been 'discovered' in bed, by moving a curtain on the
main stage, or, as Bawcutt suggests, the bed may have been pushed out
on to the stage, as in Middleton's *A Chaste Maid in Cheapside*, III.ii:
'A bed thrust out upon the stage; Allwit's wife in it.'

Malice, or any treachery beside,   10
Would stoop to my bent brows; why, I hold fate
Clasped in my fist, and could command the course
Of time's eternal motion, hadst thou been
One thought more steady than an ebbing sea.
And what? You'll now be honest, that's resolved?   15

ANNABELLA
Brother, dear brother, know what I have been,
And know that now there's but a dining-time
'Twixt us and our confusion: let's not waste
These precious hours in vain and useless speech.
Alas, these gay attires were not put on   20
But to some end; this sudden solemn feast
Was not ordained to riot in expense;
I, that have now been chambered here alone,
Barred of my guardian, or of any else,
Am not for nothing at an instant freed   25
To fresh access. Be not deceived, my brother,
This banquet is an harbinger of death
To you and me; resolve yourself it is,
And be prepared to welcome it.

GIOVANNI   Well, then;
The schoolmen teach that all this globe of earth   30
Shall be consumed to ashes in a minute.

ANNABELLA
So I have read too.

GIOVANNI   But 'twere somewhat strange
To see the waters burn; could I believe
This might be true, I could believe as well
There might be hell or Heaven.

ANNABELLA   That's most certain.   35

GIOVANNI
A dream, a dream! Else in this other world
We should know one another.

ANNABELLA   So we shall.

GIOVANNI
Have you heard so?

ANNABELLA   For certain.

17 *dining* Q *a.c.*; dying Q *b.c.*
30 *schoolmen* mediaeval theologians

11–12 *I hold fate* etc. Cf. Marlowe, *Tamburlaine*, Part I, 369–70:
            I hold the Fates bound fast in yron chaines,
            And with my hand turne Fortunes wheel about . . .

GIOVANNI   But d'ee think
  That I shall see you there?—You look on me?
  May we kiss one another, prate or laugh,   40
  Or do as we do here?
ANNABELLA   I know not that.
  But good, for the present, what d'ee mean
  To free yourself from danger? Some way think
  How to escape; I'm sure the guests are come.
GIOVANNI
  Look up, look here; what see you in my face?   45
ANNABELLA
  Distraction and a troubled countenance.
GIOVANNI
  Death, and a swift repining wrath—yet look,
  What see you in mine eyes?
ANNABELLA   Methinks you weep.
GIOVANNI
  I do indeed; these are the funeral tears
  Shed on your grave; these furrowed up my cheeks   50
  When first I loved and knew not how to woo.
  Fair Annabella, should I here repeat
  The story of my life, we might lose time.
  Be record all the spirits of the air,
  And all things else that are, that day and night,   55
  Early and late, the tribute which my heart
  Hath paid to Annabella's sacred love
  Hath been these tears, which are her mourners now.
  Never till now did Nature do her best
  To show a matchless beauty to the world,   60
  Which in an instant, ere it scarce was seen,
  The jealous Destinies required again.
  Pray, Annabella, pray; since we must part,
  Go thou, white in thy soul, to fill a throne
  Of innocence and sanctity in Heaven.   65
  Pray, pray, my sister.
ANNABELLA   Then I see your drift—
  Ye blessed angels, guard me.
GIOVANNI   So say I.
  Kiss me. If ever after-times should hear
  Of our fast-knit affections, though perhaps
  The laws of conscience and of civil use   70

42 *good* i.e. good brother
51 *woo* Q *a.c.*; woe Q *b.c.*
62 *required* Q *a.c.*; require Q *b.c.*

May justly blame us, yet when they but know
Our loves, that love will wipe away that rigour
Which would in other incests be abhorred.
Give me your hand; how sweetly life doth run
In these well-coloured veins. How constantly   75
These palms do promise health. But I could chide
With Nature for this cunning flattery.
Kiss me again—forgive me.
ANNABELLA   With my heart.
GIOVANNI
   Farewell.
ANNABELLA Will you be gone?
GIOVANNI   Be dark, bright sun,
   And make this midday night, that thy gilt rays   80
   May not behold a deed will turn their splendour
   More sooty than the poets feign their Styx.
   One other kiss, my sister.
ANNABELLA   What means this?
GIOVANNI
   To save thy fame, and kill thee in a kiss.   *Stabs her*
   Thus die, and die by me, and by my hand.   85
   Revenge is mine; honour doth love command.
ANNABELLA
   O brother, by your hand?
GIOVANNI   When thou art dead
   I'll give my reasons for't; for to dispute
   With thy (even in thy death) most lovely beauty,
   Would make me stagger to perform this act,   90
   Which I most glory in.
ANNABELLA
   Forgive him, Heaven—and me my sins; farewell.
   Brother unkind, unkind!—Mercy, great Heaven—O!—O!—
                                                    Dies
GIOVANNI
   She's dead, alas, good soul. The hapless fruit
   That in her womb received its life from me   95
   Hath had from me a cradle and a grave.
   I must not dally. This sad marriage-bed,
   In all her best, bore her alive and dead.
   Soranzo, thou hast missed thy aim in this;
   I have prevented now thy reaching plots,   100

93 *unkind* both 'cruel' and 'unnatural'   94 *hapless* luckless
100 *prevented* forestalled   100 *reaching* cunning

And killed a love, for whose each drop of blood
I would have pawned my heart. Fair Annabella,
How over-glorious art thou in thy wounds,
Triumphing over infamy and hate!
Shrink not, courageous hand, stand up, my heart,   105
And boldly act my last and greater part.

Exit with the body

[Act V, Scene vi]

A Banquet. Enter CARDINAL, FLORIO, DONADO, SORANZO,
RICHARDETTO, VASQUES, *and Attendants; they take their places*

VASQUES
   Remember, sir, what you have to do; be wise and resolute.
SORANZO
   Enough—my heart is fixed.—Pleaseth your grace
   To taste these coarse confections; though the use
   Of such set entertainments more consists
   In custom than in cause, yet, reverend sir,   5
   I am still made your servant by your presence.
CARDINAL
   And we your friend.
SORANZO
   But where's my brother Giovanni?

Enter GIOVANNI *with a heart upon his dagger*

GIOVANNI
   Here, here, Soranzo; trimmed in reeking blood,
   That triumphs over death; proud in the spoil   10
   Of love and vengeance! Fate or all the powers
   That guide the motions of immortal souls
   Could not prevent me.
CARDINAL
   What means this?
FLORIO
   Son Giovanni!   15
SORANZO
   Shall I be forestalled?
GIOVANNI
   Be not amazed; if your misgiving hearts
   Shrink at an idle sight, what bloodless fear
   Of coward passion would have seized your senses,
   Had you beheld the rape of life and beauty   20
   Which I have acted? My sister, O my sister.

FLORIO
  Ha! What of her?
GIOVANNI   The glory of my deed
  Darkened the midday sun, made noon as night.
  You came to feast, my lords, with dainty fare;
  I came to feast too, but I digged for food   25
  In a much richer mine than gold or stone
  Of any value balanced; 'tis a heart,
  A heart, my lords, in which is mine entombed:
  Look well upon't; d'ee know't?
VASQUES
  What strange riddle's this?   30
GIOVANNI
  'Tis Annabella's heart, 'tis; why d'ee startle?
  I vow 'tis hers: this dagger's point ploughed up
  Her fruitful womb, and left to me the fame
  Of a most glorious executioner.
FLORIO
  Why, madman, art thyself?   35
GIOVANNI
  Yes, father; and that times to come may know
  How as my fate I honoured my revenge,
  List, father, to your ears I will yield up
  How much I have deserved to be your son.
FLORIO
  What is't thou say'st?
GIOVANNI   Nine moons have had their changes   40
  Since I first throughly viewed and truly loved
  Your daughter and my sister.
FLORIO   How!—Alas,
  My lords, he's a frantic madman!
GIOVANNI   Father, no.
  For nine months' space in secret I enjoyed
  Sweet Annabella's sheets; nine months I lived   45
  A happy monarch of her heart and her.
  Soranzo, thou know'st this; thy paler cheek
  Bears the confounding print of thy disgrace,
  For her too fruitful womb too soon bewrayed
  The happy passage of our stol'n delights,   50
  And made her mother to a child unborn.
CARDINAL
  Incestuous villain!
FLORIO   O, his rage belies him.

GIOVANNI
  It does not, 'tis the oracle of truth;
  I vow it is so.
SORANZO   I shall burst with fury.
  Bring the strumpet forth.   55
VASQUES
  I shall, sir.   *Exit* VASQUES
GIOVANNI   Do, sir.—Have you all no faith
  To credit yet my triumphs? Here I swear
  By all that you call sacred, by the love
  I bore my Annabella whilst she lived,
  These hands have from her bosom ripped this heart.   60

Enter VASQUES

  Is't true or no, sir?
VASQUES   'Tis most strangely true.
FLORIO
  Cursed man!—Have I lived to—   *Dies*
CARDINAL   Hold up, Florio.—
  Monster of children, see what thou hast done,
  Broke thy old father's heart. Is none of you
  Dares venture on him?
GIOVANNI   Let 'em.—O, my father,   65
  How well his death becomes him in his griefs!
  Why, this was done with courage; now survives
  None of our house but I, gilt in the blood
  Of a fair sister and a hapless father.
SORANZO
  Inhuman scorn of men, hast thou a thought   70
  T'outlive thy murders?
GIOVANNI   Yes, I tell thee, yes;
  For in my fists I bear the twists of life.
  Soranzo, see this heart, which was thy wife's;
  Thus I exchange it royally for thine,   [*Stabs him*]
  And thus and thus. Now brave revenge is mine.   75
VASQUES
  I cannot hold any longer.—You, sir, are you grown insolent
  in your butcheries? Have at you!   [*They*] *fight*
GIOVANNI
  Come, I am armed to meet thee.

---

72 *twists of life.* The Parcae, in Greek mythology, spun the threads of
   mortal life, and cut them at the moment appointed for death.

VASQUES

No, will it not be yet? If this will not, another shall. Not yet?
I shall fit you anon.—Vengeance!   80

Enter BANDITTI [*and fight* GIOVANNI]

GIOVANNI

Welcome, come more of you whate'er you be,
I dare your worst—
O, I can stand no longer! Feeble arms,
Have you so soon lost strength?

VASQUES

Now you are welcome, sir!—Away, my masters, all is done,   85
shift for yourselves. Your reward is your own; shift for
yourselves.

BANDITTI

Away, away!   *Exeunt* BANDITTI

VASQUES

How d'ee, my lord; see you this? How is't?

SORANZO

Dead; but in death well pleased that I have lived   90
To see my wrongs revenged on that black devil.
O Vasques, to thy bosom let me give
My last of breath; let not that lecher live—O!—   *Dies*

VASQUES

The reward of peace and rest be with him, my ever dearest
lord and master.   95

GIOVANNI

Whose hand gave me this wound?

VASQUES

Mine, sir, I was your first man; have you enough?

GIOVANNI

I thank thee; thou hast done for me but what
I would have else done on myself. Art sure
Thy lord is dead?   100

VASQUES

O impudent slave! As sure as I am sure to see thee die.

CARDINAL

Think on thy life and end, and call for mercy.

GIOVANNI

Mercy? Why, I have found it in this justice.

CARDINAL

Strive yet to cry to Heaven.

80 *Vengeance.* This is the watchword mentioned at V.iv, 14.
101 *thee* ed. the Q

GIOVANNI   O, I bleed fast.
  Death, thou art a guest long looked for; I embrace   105
  Thee and thy wounds; O, my last minute comes!
  Where'er I go, let me enjoy this grace,
  Freely to view my Annabella's face.   *Dies*

DONADO
  Strange miracle of justice!

CARDINAL
  Raise up the city; we shall be murdered all.   110

VASQUES
  You need not fear, you shall not; this strange task being
  ended, I have paid the duty to the son which I have vowed to
  the father.

CARDINAL
  Speak, wretched villain, what incarnate fiend
  Hath led thee on to this?   115

VASQUES
  Honesty, and pity of my master's wrongs; for know, my
  lord, I am by birth a Spaniard, brought forth my country
  in my youth by Lord Soranzo's father, whom whilst he lived
  I served faithfully; since whose death I have been to this
  man as I was to him. What I have done was duty, and I   120
  repent nothing but that the loss of my life had not ransomed
  his.

CARDINAL
  Say, fellow, know'st thou any yet unnamed
  Of counsel in this incest?

VASQUES
  Yes, an old woman, sometimes guardian to this murdered   125
  lady.

CARDINAL
  And what's become of her?

VASQUES
  Within this room she is; whose eyes, after her confession, I
  caused to be put out, but kept alive, to confirm what from
  Giovanni's own mouth you have heard. Now, my lord, what   130
  I have done you may judge of, and let your own wisdom be
  a judge in your own reason.

CARDINAL
  Peace!—First this woman, chief in these effects:

125 *sometimes* formerly

---

133 *this woman*. Ambiguous; the reference might be either to Putana, or the
    dead body of Annabella.

My sentence is, that forthwith she be ta'en
Out of the city, for example's sake,   135
There to be burnt to ashes.
DONADO   'Tis most just.
CARDINAL
  Be it your charge, Donado, see it done.
DONADO
  I shall.
VASQUES
  What for me? If death, 'tis welcome; I have been honest to
  the son as I was to the father.   140
CARDINAL
  Fellow, for thee, since what thou didst was done
  Not for thyself, being no Italian,
  We banish thee forever, to depart
  Within three days; in this we do dispense
  With grounds of reason, not of thine offence.   145
VASQUES
  'Tis well; this conquest is mine, and I rejoice that a Spaniard
  outwent an Italian in revenge.   *Exit* VASQUES
CARDINAL
  Take up these slaughtered bodies, see them buried;
  And all the gold and jewels, or whatsoever,
  Confiscate by the canons of the church,   150
  We seize upon to the Pope's proper use.
RICHARDETTO [*discovers himself*]
  Your grace's pardon: thus long I lived disguised
  To see the effect of pride and lust at once
  Brought both to shameful ends.
CARDINAL
  What, Richardetto whom we thought for dead?   155
DONADO
  Sir, was it you—
RICHARDETTO   Your friend.
CARDINAL   We shall have time
  To talk at large of all; but never yet
  Incest and murder have so strangely met.
  Of one so young, so rich in nature's store,
  Who could not say, 'tis pity she's a whore?   *Exeunt* 160

FINIS

[The Printer's Apology]

The general commendation deserved by the actors in their presentment of this tragedy may easily excuse such few faults as are escaped
in the printing. A common charity may allow him the ability of
spelling whom a secure confidence assures that he cannot ignorantly
err in the application of sense.

*Printed in Great Britain by The Garden City Press Limited
Letchworth, Hertfordshire*